Japan's Dilemmas and Solutions

15 Topics You Need to Consider

考えよう日本の論点 15

by

James M. Vardaman
KAMATA Akiko
OKADA Hiroki
KOBAYASHI Ryoichiro

JN034085

TSURUMI SHOTEN

Japan's Dilemmas and Solutions:
15 Topics You Need to Consider

Photo credits:
p. 1 © Yasu / PIXTA（ピクスタ）
p. 7 © maroke / PIXTA（ピクスタ）
p. 13 © jessie / PIXTA（ピクスタ）
p. 19 © Fast&Slow / PIXTA（ピクスタ）
p. 25 © poosan / PIXTA（ピクスタ）
p. 31 Wikimedia Commons/Пресс-служба Президента Российской Федерации
p. 37 Wikimedia Commons/Fukushima nuclear power plant
p. 43 © IYO / PIXTA（ピクスタ）
p. 49 © bee / PIXTA（ピクスタ）
p. 55 © Syda Productionso / PIXTA（ピクスタ）
p. 67 © structuresxx / PIXTA（ピクスタ）
p. 73 © IYO / PIXTA（ピクスタ）
p. 79 © ijeab / PIXTA（ピクスタ）
p. 85 © SeventyFour / PIXTA（ピクスタ）

表紙／扉 © IYO / PIXTA（ピクスタ）

自習用音声について

本書の自習用音声は以下よりダウンロードできます。予習、復習に
ご利用ください。
（2023 年 4 月 1 日開始予定）

http://www.otowatsurumi.com/0056/

URL はブラウザのアドレスバーに直接入力して下さい。

はしがき

　本書の本文は、いま日本が抱えている問題を 15 とりあげ、その背景や現状を説明し、読者が問題の認識とその解決策や将来への展望を自分で考えることを意図したものです。

　日本の停滞が言われだしてから久しくなります。失われた 10 年とか、失われた 20 年とか、ことばの響きは情緒的ですが、日本は元気をなかなか取り戻せないでいるのが現実でしょう。そんな日本に COVID-19 のパンデミックはさらに追い打ちをかけ、国民の生活は不自由さを増し、価値観の変更さえも促され、パンデミック以前の世の中に戻ることはもうないだろうとも言われるようになりました。しかし、このパンデミックは私たちが日頃あまり関心を持たないでいたり、気がつかないでいたことについて考えさせる機会や時間を与えることにもなりました。

　さて、本書の眼目である「今の日本がどのような問題を抱えているのか、その認識と将来の展望を考える」ことを英語で読むメリットは何でしょうか。それは、まず第一に、日本語で読んだのではつい読み流してしまうような内容でも、英語で読むことによって、じっくりと自分の頭で考えながら読むことになる、ということでしょう。第二には時事的な英語のボキャブラリーや言い回しを覚えることが出来て、インターネットなどでニュース記事を読むのにも大いに役立つことになる、ということです。英語で日本のことを話す機会は、パンデミック後の世界で増えていくことでしょう。みずからの国が抱えている問題を率直に海外の人と話すことができるようになれば、お互いの信頼関係はずっと深まることと思います。

　英語の教科書としての実効性を持たすために、本書は各本文を 3 つのブロックに分けて各ブロックごとに英文が理解できているかをチェックする設問があります。各章末には英語の総合力を養うための文法問題とリスニング問題もつけてあります。ディスカッションのための設問も用意しましたので、授業活性化に役立てて頂ければ幸いです。

　本書が、学生の皆さんが英語を通して自分の頭で考える力を鍛える一助になることを著者として心から願っています。

2022 年 11 月

James M. Vardaman

Contents

Educational *Sakoku*

コロナ禍で日本への留学生や留学希望者たちは、政府の厳しい入国制限措置のあおりをまともに受けてしまった。日本留学を考えていた若者たちは留学先を規制のゆるい国に変更するのも選択肢の一つになっただろう。また、コロナ禍以前からであるが、日本から海外に留学する学生数が減少傾向にあることが懸念されている。学生の国際交流は大局的に見れば世界各国の文化や価値観を共有するのに重要な役割を担う。入って来る学生、出ていく学生を増やすことは国際国家として生きるために不可欠なことではないだろうか。

Educational *Sakoku*

1

    In the early seventeenth century, the Tokugawa shogunate began to view Christianity as a menace to its survival. The shogunate heard reports of how the Portuguese and the Spanish were spreading Christianity across the world and taking political control over other countries, including several in Asia. Determined to prevent that from happening to Japan, the shogunate closed Japan's borders. Japanese were 5 prohibited from traveling abroad and foreigners were permitted to visit only a few ports, including Dejima in Nagasaki harbor. This period of isolation came to be known as *sakoku*, or "closed country." It was not until Western warships sailed into Japanese waters in the mid-nineteenth century that Japan "opened" again.

    Throughout the current pandemic, Japan has implemented some of the most 10 restrictive border controls of any democratic country. But what some people have called *neo-sakoku* is different from the Tokugawa version. This new system has allowed Japanese citizens to come and go with few limits, as long as PCR tests are negative. But until recently, restrictions have barred tourists except in group tours, which can be monitored. 15

●NOTES●

1 **the Tokugawa shogunate**「徳川幕府」／ 2 **menace**「脅威」／ 4 **several** = several countries ／ 4 **Determined to prevent … closed Japan's borders.** 分詞構文。Determined … to Japan はコンマ以下の付帯状況を表す。「…することに決めて」／ 6 **a few ports** 長崎、対馬、薩摩藩の支配下にあった琉球、北海道の松前では交易がおこなわれていた。／ 8 **It was not until … that Japan "opened" again**. ここの強調構文は要注意。／ 10 **the current pandemic** 2020 年から始まった COVID19 ウィルスの世界的大流行のこと。／ 12 *neo-sakoku*「『ネオ鎖国』」neo- は「新…」を表す連結形。ne- も同じ。／ 13 **allowed Japanese citizens to come and go** allow ~ to …「~が…をするのを許す、可能にする」／ 13 **PCR test** Polymerase Chain Reaction test の略。病原体の遺伝子を増幅させることで病原体を検出、特定をする検査。／ 14 **negative**「陰性」cf. positive「陽性」／ 14 **restrictions**「規制」

✱*Comprehension Check*✱

1. Hearing that the Spanish and Portuguese were promoting Christianity . . .
   a. Japanese were sent abroad to check on reports.
   b. the shogunate stopped all foreigners from entering Japan.
   c. the Tokugawa shogunate prevented traveling abroad.

2. Current border restrictions . . .
   a. let citizens of Japan travel overseas.
   b. do not allow tour groups to enter the country.
   c. are not monitoring tourists in groups.

Japan's restrictions on foreigners—even those with permanent residence—have had a serious impact on students from abroad. In the decade ending in 2019, the number of foreign students eager to study in Japan doubled. In 2019 some 120,000 foreign students were allowed to enter Japan to study in a variety of educational institutions. Then when the pandemic began, Japan closed its doors. In 2021 only ₅ 11,600 managed to reach Japanese shores. Even foreign students who had been accepted by Japanese institutions were unable to enter the country. Some were able to take online courses from Japanese institutions, but that is not the same as living in Japan, meeting Japanese people, and experiencing Japanese culture.

Foreign students who have been unable to reach Japan to study have been left ₁₀ with two options. One is to wait and wonder when the doors will open. The other is to give up and look for another country with fewer restrictions.

Closing the doors to foreign students may seem like a short-term gain for controlling the spread of the pandemic in Japan. But if Japanese citizens can come and go, why not allow foreign students who are vaccinated and can pass a PCR test? ₁₅ These students are no higher risk than Japanese citizens. This hesitancy to let them in suggests that at least some portion of the population sees coronavirus as a foreign menace, rather than a pandemic that is spreading among Japanese as well.

● NOTES ●

1 **those** = those people／1 **permanent residence**「永住権」／2 **decade** = ten years／3 **some** = about／
5 **Japan closed its doors**「入国を禁止した」。doors はこの場合出入りをする場所を意味する。／6 **manage to**「どうにか…する」／13 **Closing the doors to foreign students** Closing は動名詞。Closing … students までが主語／13 **short-term gain**「短期利益、目先の利益」／16 **to let them in** 副詞句形容詞的用法。hesitancy を修飾する。／17 **sees coronavirus as a foreign menace** see 〜 as …「〜を…とみなす」

✳ *Comprehension Check* ✳

3. The number of students from abroad . . .
   a. doubled in one year.
   b. was ten times more in 2019 than in 2021.
   c. increased due to economic factors.

4. Stopping foreign students from coming to Japan . . .
   a. has been an effective means of stopping the spread of the pandemic.
   b. has encouraged students to be more interested in Japan.
   c. has stopped them from experiencing life in Japan.

3

In the long run, Japan benefits from having foreign students come to its language schools, colleges, and research institutes. They often become bridge-builders between Japan and their home countries. They learn from Japan, make friends, and explain their own country's culture to the Japanese.

Also of concern, not necessarily related to the pandemic, is the decline in the number of Japanese students interested in studying abroad. From the late 1980s to early 2000s, the number of Japanese seeking degrees overseas rocketed. But times have changed. According to the education ministry only 4% of all university students study abroad. In 2019 a government survey found that only a third of Japanese want to study abroad, compared with 66% of South Koreans and 51% of Germans.

Some commentators explain this by pointing to conservative employers who are not interested in recruiting students who have been abroad. Others claim it is the students' lack of foreign language ability that prevents them from gaining entrance to schools. For others, the cost of studying abroad is beyond the means of family budgets. Whatever the main reasons may be, this is also a loss over the long term.

Japanese enterprises are no longer the dynamic force they were in the 1980s. The days of "Japan as Number One" are past. The businesses, research institutes, and the public in general need new ideas, varieties of connections, and expanded networks. Students coming in and going abroad are key to meeting these needs.

●NOTES●

1 **in the long run**「長期的には、結局は」／1 **having foreign students come** have+O+原形。許容を表す「～に…させる、～に…してもらう」／2 **bridge-builder**「懸け橋、橋渡しをする人」／5 **Also of concern, not necessarily related to the pandemic, is the decline in the number of Japanese students interested in studying abroad** The decline in the number of Japanese students interested in studying abroad is of concern. の倒置表現。not necessarily related to the pandemic は挿入。not necessarily「必ずしも…ではない」部分否定／5 **relate to**「…に関連する」／7 **rocket**「急上昇する」同義語に skyrocket.／8 **the education ministry** = Ministry of Education, Science, Sports and Culture「文部科学省」／12 **it is the students' lack of foreign language ability that** 文頭の it は仮主語で that 以下を指す。／14 **means**「財力、資力」／16 **enterprise**「企業」

Comprehension Check

5. In 2019 the number of university students wanting to study abroad . . .
   a. was larger in South Korea than in Germany.
   b. was roughly 50% in Japan.
   c. was unaffected by family finances.

❅ Structure Practice ❅

A. Choose the one underlined word or phrase that should be corrected or rewritten. Then change it so that the sentence is correct.

1. ₁<u>Restricting</u> entrance of foreign students has had an ₂<u>affect</u> on the plans of young people ₃<u>eager</u> to live in Japan and ₄<u>attend</u> its universities. [   ]

2. In ₁<u>the long term</u>, every nation ₂<u>benefit</u> by sending students ₃<u>abroad</u> and ₄<u>receiving</u> students from other countries. [   ]

B. Choose the word or phrase that best completes the sentence.

3. It is often said that . . . success is to be ready from the start.
   a. the entrance to   b. the force to   c. the answer to   d. the key to

4. When someone is hesitant to speak in public, that person is not . . . to give presentations.
   a. seeking   b. eager   c. allowed   d. monitored

5. Because tuitions of universities are . . . , fewer students can afford to attend without doing part-time jobs in their spare time.
   a. rocketing   b. menacing   c. restricting   d. preventing

❅ Listening Challenge ❅

Listen and fill in the missing words.
4

1. In ¹[   ] generations, foreigners who came to Japan ²[
   ] literature, culture, and martial arts, but ³[   ], the attraction
   has been anime, manga, and pop culture.

2. Students who ¹[   ] tend to have a broader ²[   ],
   which allows them to see issues ³[   ] of view.

3. One common pathway ¹[   ] Japan for several years ²[
          ] an assistant English language teacher, which provides many
   ³[   ] people and pays for basic living expenses.

4. Participating ¹[   ] like judo or soccer ²[   ]
   speak different languages to become friends and ³[   ] each
   other's language.

5. International exchanges ¹[   ] the growth of businesses and
   ²[   ], so governments ³[   ] such activities.

Going Further (for discussion or research)

1. In what ways do you think Japanese universities and universities abroad might be different?

2. Why would students from overseas want to study in Japan?

Impact of Lowering the Age of "Adulthood"

民法が改正され、成人年齢が 18 歳に引き下げられた。すでに選挙の投票権は 2015 年の選挙法改正で 18 歳から与えられていたが、今回の民法改正で 18 歳になると保護者の同意が無くとも自らの意思で様々な契約ができるようになった。ただ飲酒、喫煙、ギャンブルなどは従来通り禁止だ。同時にされた少年法の改正で 18、19 歳は『特定少年』と位置づけられ、刑事事件で受けられる特例が原則として適用されないことになった。18 歳になると選挙の投票権を始めとして様々な権利を行使できるようになったが、クレジットカードの安易な契約などには使いすぎによる危険が伴うことを忘れていないだろうか。

Impact of lowering the age of "adulthood"

The laws of each country distinguish between "minors" and "adults." Until minors—more commonly called children—reach the age of adulthood, they are under the legal control and legal responsibility of their parents or guardians. When minors become a certain age, they become legally responsible for their own actions and decisions. Each country makes its own decision regarding this age, and recently Japan has made the first change in more than 140 years. In part, this move aims at encouraging young Japanese between the ages of 18 and 20 to become socially responsible earlier.

Japan's Civil Code was revised on April 1, 2022, changing the legal definition of an adult. The age of adulthood was previously set at 20, but now Japanese between the ages of 18 and 20 have new freedoms, as well as new responsibilities. And considerable attention has been given to the issue of whether they are ready to take on these responsibilities. And if these younger adults are not yet prepared, how should society help them become adequately prepared?

●NOTES●

title **adulthood**「成人」成人年齢は国ごとに異なり、プエルトリコやハイチは14歳、スコットランドは16歳、イギリス、フランス、ロシア、オランダなどは18歳、韓国は19歳、アルゼンチン、インドネシアは21歳から成人。アメリカは州によって異なる。／1 **distinguish between … and …**「…と…を区別する」／3 **guardian**「後見人」／4 **responsible for …**「…に対して責任がある」／6 **the first change in more than 140 years** the first … in …「…ぶりに…」cf. I heard from my friend in America for the first time in two years.「アメリカの友人から2年ぶりに便りがあった」／9 **Civil Code**「民法」／9 **revise**「改正する」

✱ *Comprehension Check* ✱

1. In various countries, the laws regarding the age of adulthood . . .
   a. give legal responsibility for minors to parents or guardians
   b. depend upon the actions of the children.
   c. have no effect on individual responsibility.

2. Beginning in 2022, . . .
   a. Japanese became responsible as adults at the age of 20.
   b. younger adults were given new rights.
   c. the number of young adults decreased.

One of the earliest subjects of debate in this issue was that of legal responsibility. Until this change in the law, criminal offenders between the ages of 18 and 20 were not tried as adults. They were referred to family courts and tried as minors. Their names and faces were kept out of the media by law. This was intended to protect young offenders from being put in the public eye and to give them a second chance in life. If they were found guilty of a crime, they were sent to reformatory facilities, where they might make a fresh start. But now, people in that two-year age group will face stricter punishments as adults. Further, if they commit crimes, the media is free to disclose their names and faces in reportage.

Another issue that has gained particular attention is the possibility that 18- and 19-year-olds might become easy targets for scams. If they are not knowledgeable about personal finances, interest rates, and the need to budget expenses, they could be drawn into risky consumer contracts. Until now, parental consent was necessary for obtaining a consumer credit card, mobile phone contracts, and housing rental agreements. Parents needed to co-sign contracts. That helped them avoid financial problems. Without parental guidance, however, young adults without being aware of it could get tricked into serious financial debt.

● NOTES ●

2 **criminal offender**「犯罪者」／3 **try**「裁判する、審理する」／3 **refer to**「…に任せる」／3 **family court**「家庭裁判所」／4 **intend to**「…を意図する、…しようとする」／6 **reformatory facility**「更生施設」／7 **two-year age group** 新たに成人となる 1820 歳のグループのこと。／9 **disclose**「公表する、暴露する」／9 **reportage**「報道」／11 **scam**「詐欺」／11 **knowledgeable**「…を知っている、…についての知識がある」／12 **personal finance**「個人向け融資」／12 **interest**「金利、利子」／15 **co-sign**「連帯署名」。co- は with, together の意味を表す接頭辞。／17 **trick … into …**「…をだまして…させる」の受動態。

✳ *Comprehension Check* ✳

3. Prior to the change in Japan's Civil Code . . .

   a. young offenders between 18 and 20 were not shown in the media.

   b. offenders under the age of 20 received stricter punishments.

   c. no young offenders were sent to reformatories.

4. Contracts for mobile phones and consumer credit cards . . .

   a. for Japanese over the age of 18 require consent from parents.

   b. involve no risk for people of any age.

   c. can now be made by young adults over the age of 18.

A self-confident younger adult may not be aware of how quickly interest payments on credit cards can add up. It is great to be able to buy an attractive item by just showing a credit card, but if you don't have money to make the payment by the due date, interest is added. And that interest can pile up quickly. What seems like freedom and fun can turn into a serious struggle rather quickly. 5

At a more everyday level, these new adults have the right—and responsibility—to vote in elections for people to represent their communities. Until now, schools tiptoed around political issues. They focused on textbook materials and what might be on examinations. But now some schools, teachers, and student groups have taken initiative in researching and discussing various issues of importance today. By doing 10 this, they prepare younger adults to make responsible decisions in the voting booth.

Although the legal definition of adulthood has changed, it does not change prohibitions from drinking alcohol, the purchase of cigarettes, or gambling. Those restrictions remain until the age of 20.

However, they will be able to apply for passports without parental permission. 15 They will be able to apply for national licenses for certain businesses. And they will be eligible to serve on juries. Given that many adults are not eager to take on the responsibility of serving on a jury in a court trial, it will be interesting to see whether the younger generation will take a different approach.

●NOTES●

1 **be aware of**「…に気が付く」／ 2 **add up**「積もり積もって大きな量になる」／ 4 **pile up**「蓄積する、積み上がる」／ 8 **tiptoe around**「…を避ける」／ 10 **initiative**「主導権」／ 11 **voting booth**「投票用紙記入所」／ 17 **eligible to**「…の資格がある」／ 17 **given**「…を考慮すれば、…を考えると」cf. Given her age, she did very well.「彼女の年齢を考慮すると、かなりよくやった方だ」

✱ *Comprehension Check* ✱

5. The new legal definition of adulthood in Japan . . .

   a. enables people over the age of 18 to purchase alcohol.

   b. allows people over 18 to make an application for a passport.

   c. requires that everyone between 18 and 20 serve on a jury.

❈ Structure Practice ❈

A. Choose the one underlined word or phrase that should be corrected or rewritten. Then change it so that the sentence is correct.

1. One central issue seems to be ₁if 18-year-olds are ₂capable of making responsible decisions ₃regarding contracts involving ₄personal finance.   [   ]

2. ₁Unless one is aware of ₂the risks of using credit cards, interest could ₃grow up much more quickly than ₄anticipated.   [   ]

B. Choose the word or phrase that best completes the sentence.

3. Adults are required to . . . responsibility for their actions.
   a. initiate   b. put   c. take   d. understand

4. When one "tiptoes" around a subject, one tries to . . . .
   a. do it quietly   b. treat it with caution
   c. move slowly   d. make it quick

5. Prior to climbing a mountain overnight, it is essential to be . . . prepared.
   a. adequately   b. legally   c. quickly   d. recently

❈ Listening Challenge ❈

🎧 **Listen and fill in the missing words.**
8

1. Defining adulthood and ¹[   ] to a whole population is difficult, because people mature ²[   ], depending on how they were raised, what their families expected, and ³[   ] responsibilities as children.

2. Children ¹[   ] an allowance once a week or ²[   ] tend to learn how to plan their purchases and learn ³[   ] items they really want.

3. Punishment for those ¹[   ] often takes ²[   ]
   the age, the motive, and the future of the person ³[   ].

4. Certain political issues ¹[   ] for young people to grasp, but it
   is important to gradually ²[   ] the issues at their own level
   ³[   ].

5. It ¹[   ] that a small percentage ²[   ] with
   new ideas and skills will ³[   ] their own businesses.

Going Further (for discussion or research)

1. How would you define a "mature adult," without considering a particular age?

2. Imagine that you have graduated from university and are living by yourself.
   Approximately how much would your annual living costs be?

Remote or In-person?
Benefits and Disadvantages

コロナ禍は様ざまな分野に影響を及ぼし、会社ではリモートワークを推進し、大学においてはほとんどの授業がリモートで行われるほどであった。通勤するストレスから解放されても、一日中家庭で仕事をしていればまた違ったストレスがたまることだろう。大学の授業でも効率的な授業が出来るかもしれないが、パソコンを使う技術が未熟な先生はいるだろうし、何よりも学生からは折角の大学生活における仲間との語らいや先生との交流の機会を奪うことになる。しかし、好むと好まざるにかかわらず、これからますます増えていくであろうリモートの世界のメリットを積極的に考える必要があるのかもしれない。

Remote or In-person? Benefits and Disadvantages

The COVID-19 pandemic has influenced the business and education worlds in many ways. From school age to work retirement age, almost everyone has been affected. Let us first look at the world of business.

Undoubtedly the largest impact has been the switch to having employees working remotely at least some weekdays. For businesses, long accustomed to having all their employees in one location, with direct supervision by managers, this has been a major challenge.

Accomplishing remote working requires, of course, a stable broadband internet connection and all of the necessary computer equipment in the remote location. Any technical failure or a break in the connection can cause major problems for workers logging into their company databases or holding meetings on platforms such as Zoom. Remote connections also present challenges to security measures.

The upside for most employees is the reduction in stress that results from long commutes on crowded trains, especially with the potential spread of the virus in crowds. Workers can sleep a bit longer, take a little more time getting ready to start work, dress casually, and avoid irritating coworkers in the elevators at the office. Perhaps the most positive advantage is not having their work interrupted by constant phone calls during the day.

● NOTES ●

title **in-person**「生の、実況の」。この場合は remote「遠隔」に対する「対面」の意味。／1 **The COVID-19** 2019 年 12 月に初の感染例が確認され、世界的な大流行を引き起こした新型コロナウイルス感染症。／1 **pandemic**「世界的流行の」。pan-「全…、汎…」(cf. Pan-American「全米の」, Pan-Pacific「汎太平洋の」) dem「民衆、大衆」(cf. democracy「民主主義」) -ic「…の、…のような」(cf. academic「学問の、学術的な」) cf. endemic「特定の地域やグループに特有の」(endemic disease「風土病」), epidemic「流行性の」(全国的、全世界的など、影響範囲がより広いものを pandemic と呼ぶ)／5 **long accustomed to having all their employees in one location, with direct supervision by managers,** 形容詞句。businesses を修飾する。／5 **accustomed to**「…に慣れている」／8 **Accomplishing remote working** 動名詞句。requires の主語。／11 **platform**「プラットホーム」。この場合はシステムやサービスの土台や基盤となる環境のこと。／12 **Zoom** アメリカ Zoom ビデオコミュニケーションズが開発、提供する、オンライン上でミーティングができる Web 会議システム。／13 **upside** =merit, advantage／16 **irritating** 形容詞。coworkers を修飾する。

✸ *Comprehension Check* ✸

1. One major impact of COVID-19 has been that . . .

   a. every employee in many companies never comes to the office.

   b. some companies have all of their employees working remotely.

   c. many companies have employees work remotely at least one day a week.

2. Among the drawbacks of working remotely is . . .

    a. the possibility of technical problems with computers.

    b. not being able to get enough sleep at night.

    c. being interrupted by many phone calls during working hours.

10

    The downside is being stuck at home all day. If they have children who are also at home all day, then they have to deal with their own work and their children's demands. And despite their previous complaints about "the office," they miss the camaraderie of friends at work and going out to lunch together.

    Even when restrictions are eventually lifted and in-office work becomes more   5 common, there is another issue to consider: how many days a week should people go to the office? Already there is speculation that employees will want at least one day a week away from the office. The leading candidate according to informal surveys is Wednesday. On the other hand, working at home is just too lonely for the majority, so employees probably will want to come to their offices at least once in a while, for 10 the camaraderie. While it is hard to predict exactly how things in the workplace will change, it is safe to say that there will not be a full return to the previous "normal."

●NOTES●

1 **downside** =demerit, disadvantage ／4 **camaraderie**「仲間意識」／5 **lift**「（規制などを）なくす、撤廃する」／8 **leading candidate**「有力候補」。前文の one day a week away from the office のことを指す。／ 8 **The leading candidate according to informal surveys is Wednesday** = According to the result of informal surveys, Wednesday is the leading candidate. ／ 10 **once in a while**「時折」／ 11 **it is hard to predict exactly how things in the workplace will change**　it は形式主語。真主語は to 以下。how … は predict の目的語。

✻ Comprehension Check ✻

3. Working remotely from home . . .

    a. has several disadvantages.

    b. allows more free time with coworkers at lunchtime.

    c. is better than working at the office in every way.

4. In the future, whether most employees will be in the office full time or not . . .

    a. depends on the season.

    b. is difficult to predict.

    c. is completely unlikely.

11
 In the world of education, from elementary school to university, the pandemic has clearly altered how and where students learn and how instructors teach. From both sides—that of learners and teachers—there is a significant difference between face-to-face contact and distance learning via a computer monitor.

 First of all, together in a classroom, it is possible for a teacher to give more 5 individual instruction to those who seem to need it. Handing out printed materials is easier. Using a large white board, adding explanations when students look somewhat puzzled, and answering questions along the way is easier. In a remote session, students may be distracted by what is going on in their home and may not feel at ease in delaying classwork by asking questions. 10

 Teaching remotely is especially a challenge for instructors who are not technically skilled. It may be tempting to just deliver a one-way lecture, ask for questions at the end, and let that be it. This method is boring in real life; it is much more boring in remote mode.

 Schools are also social occasions, and having some give-and-take during and 15 between classes is valuable. We need casual conversation with a variety of people. We learn how other people think, we practice offering our own views, and we discover good ways to respond to others' feelings. These are not education in the narrow sense of the word, but they are skills that we will use for the rest of our lives.

● NOTES ●

2 **alter** = change ／ 11 **technically**「技術的に」。この場合は、PC や zoom などの操作のことを指す。／ 12 **tempting**「…したくなる」。後に for instructors を補って考える。／ 12 **a one-way lecture**「一方的な講義」／ 15 **give-and-take**「やり取り、意見の交換」

✳ *Comprehension Check* ✳

5. In an actual classroom, . . .

 a. classes tend to be less boring.

 b. students are more distracted by their environment.

 c. there is no opportunity to discuss ideas with other students.

❃ Structure Practice ❃

A. Choose the one underlined word or phrase that should be corrected or rewritten. Then change it so that the sentence is correct.

1. Some employees will ₁<u>prefer</u> a ₂<u>regularly</u> schedule, even if it ₃<u>combines</u> working ₄<u>partly</u> at home and the rest at the office.   [   ]

2. Although many in the audience ₁<u>found</u> her comments ₂<u>puzzled</u>, they did not feel it was ₃<u>appropriate</u> to raise their hands and ask her to explain in more ₄<u>detail</u>.

    [   ]

B. Choose the word or phrase that best completes the sentence.

3. He's nice but he has . . . habit of interrupting others in a conversation.
    a. a challenging   b. an exceptional   c. an irritating   d. a remote

4. Coworkers can provide camaraderie . . . the workplace, but they can also become troublesome if they interrupt what you are doing.
    a. about   b. during   c. over   d. within

5. "Hand out" is another way of saying . . . .
    a. demonstrate   b. distribute   c. promote   d. submit

❃ Listening Challenge ❃

🎧 **Listen and fill in the missing words.**
12

1. Some remote workers ¹[   ] they are easily distracted ²[   ], pets, and delivery personnel, and are ³[   ] because they are don't get outside.

2. Staring at a monitor during an online meeting is [1][   ] being in a room with others and [2][   ] on their faces during a [3][   ].

3. Not having [1][   ] time commuting to and from work is [2][   ] to the remote work routine, which leaves workers [3][   ] to sleep at night, too.

4. The normal give-and-take [1][   ] between classes is [2][   ] eliminated when classes are provided online and [3][   ] on a monitor.

5. The old-fashioned [1][   ], in which an instructor, stands [2][   ] a group of students and delivers a mostly one-way presentation may [3][   ] when we return to classes in person.

Going Further (for discussion or research)

1. Some contend that by looking at someone's face, one can tell whether the person is telling the truth of not. Do you believe that is true?

2. What advantages and disadvantages do you see in attending a meeting or a class remotely?

CHAPTER *4* 男女格差

Gender Equality

世界の国の男女平等度を比較した「ジェンダーギャップ指数」がスイスにある国際的な機関「世界経済フォーラム」から毎年発表される。「ジェンダーギャップ指数」は「男女平等格差指数」とも呼ばれ、教育、健康、政治、経済の分野を分析して男女が平等な状態を100％とした場合の達成率を指数化したものだ。「男女共同参画社会」の推進が言われて久しくなるが、2022 年に発表された指数では、日本は主要先進国の中で最下位に甘んじたままである。掛け声だけでない、指数改善へ繋がる具体的な方策はあるのだろうか。

Gender Equality

🎧
13

In virtually all of the studies of gender equality in the nations of the world, Japan is far and away behind the times. According to the World Economic Forum's Global Gender Gap Report in 2022, Japan ranked 116 out of 146 countries in gender equality. That leaves Japan in last place among the major advanced economies. In terms of women's political empowerment, as measured by the number of female politicians, Japan rates even lower, at 139. Among members of the OECD countries, Japan is dead last. This is quite a poor showing for one of the world's rich countries.

A Japan Foundation survey shows why so few women are going into politics. The top five factors mentioned in the survey include difficulty in balancing duties as a member of the Japanese Diet and family life, the overall attitude that politics are for men only, the lack of an environment for encouraging female politicians, and discrimination against and harassment of women politicians.

The gap between men and women is prominent in several places. In the political arena, as of August 2022, women accounted for less than 10% of lawmakers in the House of Representatives, the Lower House of the Diet, and around 25% in the House of Councilors, the Upper House. At election time, political parties promote female candidates. But this is more like window dressing than a serious attempt to balance the genders. One party proposed measures such as requiring that 15% of all the party's candidates be women and giving more top positions to women. Other parties have proposed 30% and 35% as the first step toward an ultimate target of 50%.

5

10

15

20

●NOTES●
1 **virtually**「大部分は」／2 **far and away**「断然、圧倒的に」／2 **the times**「時代」／2 **the World Economic Forum**「世界経済フォーラム (WEF)」。1971 年経済学者クラウス・シュワブにより設立された。経済、政治、学究、その他の社会におけるリーダーたちが連携することにより、世界、地域、産業の課題を形成し、世界情勢の改善に取り組むことを目的とした国際機関。／4 **advanced economy**「先進国」。この場合の economy は経済圏としての国家を指す。／6 **OECD**「経済協力開発機構」。Organization for Economic Cooperation and Development の略。／6 **dead** 強意の意味「完全な、全く」。cf. a dead silence「完全なる沈黙、全くの静寂」a dead calm「全くの無風、べた凪」／7 **showing**「出来栄え、成績」／8 **Japan Foundation**「国際交流基金」。外務省が所管する独立行政法人の一つ。／10 **Diet**「国会」／14 **the House of Representatives**「下院、（日本の）衆議院」／15 **the Lower House**「下院、（日本の）衆議院」／15 **the House of Councilors**「上院、（日本の）参議院」／16 **the Upper House**「上院、（日本の）参議院」／17 **window dressing**「体裁を繕うこと、粉飾」

�҂ *Comprehension Check* ✚

1. The Japan Foundation survey does not mention . . .
   a. work-life balance issues.
   b. harassment of female politicians.
   c. the importance of financial support.

2. In the Japanese Diet, the percentage of women . . .
   a. in the Lower House is less than that in the Upper House.
   b. is approximately the same in both houses.
   c. exceeds that of men.

Progress toward gender equality is not simply a matter of having women in the Diet or in the boardroom. It is a matter of ensuring that they have actual decision-making powers.

In the workplace, one finds *matahara*, harassment for becoming pregnant and taking maternity leave. The "inconvenience" of having a female employee go on 5 leave has multiple impacts. One is that it is used as an excuse to avoid promoting women to higher positions with heavier responsibilities. Another is that it forces more women than men into part-time, contract, or casual work. In these positions, they earn only 74% of the median male wage on average.

Given the traditional assumption that women in the workplace would "naturally" 10 also tend to all of the household duties when not at the workplace, it is doubtful whether equality of the genders will be reached there either. Men in all positions will need to step up and take on part of the responsibilities for housekeeping, childrearing, and caring for elderly family members. As of 2021, however, only about 14% of men take their statutory year's paternity leave, which would relieve women of at least a 15 portion of the burden of childrearing. When one young male Diet member actually took paternity leave, it was so unusual that it was taken up in all of the media.

●NOTES●

2 **boardroom**「重役室」／ 2 **decision-making powers**「意思決定権」。この場合の power は権限のことを意味する。／ 4 *matahara*　maternity harassment の略。／ 5 **maternity leave**「出産休暇」。leave は休暇の意味。cf. paternity leave「（父親が取る）育児休暇」(l. 15) ／ 5 **having a female employee go on leave**　have（使役動詞）＋目的語＋原形不定詞「…に…させる」。go on leave「休暇を取る」／ 8 **casual**「臨時の、不定期の」／ 10 **given**「…を考慮すれば」／ 15 **statutory**「法定の、制定法の」

� Comprehension Check ✱

3. When female employees become pregnant and take maternity leave . . .
    a. it is easy to switch to part-time work.
    b. this can result in lack of promotions.
    c. they can move ahead in their careers.

4. Japanese society, including the business world, assumes that . . .
    a. male employees will not take paternity leave.
    b. female employees will be equally promoted through their careers.
    c. men will take an active role in elderly care of family members.

15
    The government is making little progress in ensuring child-care nurseries for all parents who want to work. Without nurseries near workplaces, parents are under great pressure to drop off their young children before work starts and rush to pick them up before the nursery closes. This is hard enough for working couples, but it puts single mothers in a real bind. It continues to be a problem even when children   5
enter school. Who can take care of children after school lets out, or when they fall sick? Without a relative to help out, it is very hard to keep working.

    At the top ranks of government, there are usually only two or three women among the 20 Cabinet ministers. In the large Japanese corporations, chances are that there would not be a single woman as the CEO or board chairperson. As to how many   10
businesses are actually owned by women, in Japan that figure is a dismal 17%.

●NOTES●
2 **under great pressure**「重圧を感じる」／5 **in a real bind**「苦境に陥って、困って」／6 **let out**「(授業などが) 終わる」／6 **fall sick**「病気になる」／10 **the CEO or board chairperson**「最高経営責任者、取締役会長」。president より上位。CEO は chief executive officer の略。／11 **dismal**「惨憺たる、悲惨な」

✱ Comprehension Check ✱

5. A major concern for employees who have young children is finding . . .
    a. relatives to help out.
    b. new places to work.
    c. child-care nurseries near where they work.

❀ Structure Practice ❀

A. Choose the one underlined word or phrase that should be corrected or rewritten. Then change it so that the sentence is correct.

1. As the population ₁ages, it will be ever more important for men to ₂step over and participate in ₃carrying out household chores and ₄taking care of the elderly.

    [   ]

2. Without government ₁assistant in increasing nurseries, pressure ₂will be put on couples who both work to find dependable ₃child-care facilities that are ₄convenient to the parents' places of work.   [   ]

B. Choose the word or phrase that best completes the sentence.

3. On my way to the dentist, I'll go by the post office to . . . this package.
    a. drop in   b. drop down   c. drop off   d. drop over

4. During my illness, my coworkers had to . . . some of my duties, and I was very grateful to them.
    a. come over   b. pick up   c. take on   d. try out

5. We'll have to . . . this issue with our boss before we move forward.
    a. bring off   b. make out   c. put off   d. take up

❀ Listening Challenge ❀

🎧 **Listen and fill in the missing words.**
16

1. I came in ¹[   ] in the half-marathon, but I ²[   ] for actually finishing at all, because it was a super hot day, and I ³[   ] enough.

2. When I ¹[   ], my mother worked ²[   ], so at
   the end of the day we went out to eat at inexpensive cafeterias, so ³[
            ] cook dinner.

3. A coworker ¹[   ] on medical leave, so ²[   ] are
   dividing up his duties for the next month or so ³[   ].

4. Our work day ¹[   ] but most of us are already in the office ²[
            ], drinking coffee ³[   ] our desks.

5. It is ¹[   ] career women prefer to remain single, ²[
            ] married women are expected to do a second job after they get
   home, ³[   ] the house and the family.

Going Further (for discussion or research)

1. In what ways would Japanese society be different if every workplace was 50%
   women and 50% men?

2. Would making child care and elderly care more available have a positive impact
   on Japan as a whole?

Freedom of Speech and Its Implications

ヘイトスピーチ、フェイクニュース、ポルノなどの投稿は各 SNS の規約で禁じられている。トランプ前大統領と Twitter 社の対立で表面化した言論の自由の規制問題だが、あらたに Twitter 社を買収したイーロン・マスク氏は Twitter が利用者の主義主張をアカウント凍結やツイートの削除などで積極的に制限する姿勢を批判している。日本では主に匿名性の高い SNS による個人への誹謗中傷、いじめが問題だ。悪意で自殺に追い込まれる人間の無念さはいかばかりであろうか。言論の自由は民主主義に不可欠だが、その意味を履き違えている人間が多くいるなかで、言論の自由を守るにはどうすれば良いのだろうか。

Freedom of Speech and Its Implications

🎧
17
    Freedom of speech is so important in American culture that it is the First Amendment to the U.S. Constitution. It is the right to speak without censorship or restraint by the government. But there are limits to what one can say. Justice Oliver Wendell Holmes of the Supreme Court, for example, argued that shouting "Fire!" in a crowded theater when there was no fire, could cause unwarranted panic and danger to the   5 people inside. That, he claimed, would be an abuse of free speech.

    Most democracies in the world have similar guarantees of free speech, but they also have limitations. In social media, this has become an issue worldwide. Social media is used in a positive way to convey facts and accurate information. But to date, few restraints have been put in place to eliminate the lies and false information which   10 could have dangerous repercussions.

    Posting of hostile and defamatory messages aimed at individuals on social media has become a serious social issue around the world, and Japan is no exception. There are several distinct types of targets.

●NOTES●

1 **the First Amendment**「（アメリカ合衆国）憲法修正箇条第1条」／2 **the U.S. Constitution**「合衆国憲法」。1787年草案、88年発効。憲法典7条と修正箇条27条からなる。／2 **censorship**「検閲」／2 **restraint**「抑制、拘束」／3 **justice**「判事」／4 **the Supreme Court**「最高裁判所」／5 **unwarranted**「不当な」。un は否定の接頭辞。／6 **abuse**「濫用、悪用」／9 **to date**「現在までのところ」／10 **put in place**「実行する」／11 **repercussions**「影響」。re「…しなおす、もとへ…する」＋ percussion「響き、振動」／12 **defamatory**「中傷的な」

✳*Comprehension Check*✳

1. Freedom of speech as guaranteed in the U.S. Constitution . . .

    a. is unlimited.

    b. has some limits.

    c. should not be limited.

2. Some messages and information posted on social media . . .

    a. has become more restrained in recent years.

    b. has become very popular.

    c. has attacked individuals.

Olympian Rui Hachimura of the NBA Washington Wizards and his brother Aren Hachimura, who plays basketball for Tokai University, have been targeted on social media daily with anti-Black slurs and comments that they "should die." The brothers were born to a Beninese father and a Japanese mother, have grown up in Japan, and, naturally, speak Japanese, so they understand the comments all too well. 5 Japanese would like to think that Japan is a racism-free society, but messages on social media although written in Japanese seem like they are taken directly from a white-supremacist website.

Prior to the Tokyo Olympics, several Japanese athletes announced that they had received social media messages telling them they should pull out of the Olympics. 10 Whether the messages were specifically aimed at the athlete or at the decision to hold the Olympics and Paralympics despite the surge in Covid cases in the months leading up to the event was hard to determine. But the personal attacks by anonymous message posters is a burden no one should have to bear. The Japanese Olympic Committee had to set up a task force to shield the athletes from potentially hateful comments, but 15 social media platforms do little to stop so-called freedom of expression.

There have always been bullies. And they have shown their faces in school rooms, workplaces, and public media. In some cases, bystanders do nothing to prevent the bullying. They seem to be afraid that if they speak up and confront the bully, they will become a target, too. It takes courage to defend a victim of bullying. 20

But bullying in person is one thing; social media allows bullies to target people and organizations in a different way: anonymously. They can say nasty, cruel things without restraint, without fear of reprisal. Whatever their motivations, they must find some kind of pleasure in venting frustration by attacking others, without having to take any responsibility or face any repercussions. 25

●NOTES●

3 **slurs**「中傷」／4 **Beninese**「ベナン人の」／6 **racism-free**「人種者差別のない」。-free「…を免れた、…がない」cf. duty-free「免税の」／8 **white-supremacist**「白人至上主義者」／9 **prior to**「…より前に」／9 **the Tokyo Olympics** 定冠詞を付けること、Olympics と複数形で使うことに注意。／10 **pull out of**「撤退する、手を引く」／16 **so-called**「いわゆる」／19 **bully**「いじめ」／23 **reprisal**「報復行為」

✳ *Comprehension Check* ✳

3. It is not clear whether social media messages to some Japanese athletes prior to the Olympics . . .
   a. were generated by foreign governments.
   b. came from foreigners or from Japanese.
   c. were aimed at the decision to hold the Olympics during the pandemic.

4. Bystanders who observe bullying…
   a. may be afraid of becoming a target too.
   b. probably bully other people as well.
   c. are very courageous.

The digital age and media platforms can benefit society, but such bullying and harassment are heavy prices for some individuals to pay. If you want to use such platforms—and if you care about the responses you might get—you are setting yourself up as a possible target. It's great to receive "likes" and other kinds of encouragement, but no one likes to be put down, by anyone, especially an anonymous 5 person who enjoys attacking others.

To be sure, social media can be of great help in communicating accurate, helpful information to people who ignore traditional media like newspapers and television. But not everything communicated is accurate or helpful. Social media can spread innocuous material but can also convey disinformation, portions of which are 10 propaganda. People who read and "share" this false information are made to wonder what is true. They may believe something they read even if it is a complete lie. That is dangerous when it comes to health issues, political opinions, and social movements.

●NOTES●

1 **media platforms** メディアを通じた情報交換をできる場のことを表す。／5 **put down**「けなす、こき下ろす」／10 **innocuous**「特に害がない」in（not の意味を表す否定の接頭辞）+ nocuous「有害な」／10 **disinformation**「偽情報」。dis（false, wrong の意味を表す否定の接頭辞）+ information ／11 **are made to wonder** 使役動詞の受動態。動詞の後ろに不定詞が来ることに注意。cf. His father <u>made</u> his son <u>study</u>. → His son was <u>made to study</u> by his father.

✽ *Comprehension Check* ✽

5. The information spread on social media platforms . . .
   a. is never reliable.
   b. may be accurate.
   c. is rarely dangerous.

❋ Structure Practice ❋

A. Choose the one underlined word or phrase that should be corrected or rewritten. Then change it so that the sentence is correct.

1. $_1$Various types of social media has $_2$both negative and positive $_3$impacts on countries $_4$in the world.   [   ]

2. It $_1$takes courage to $_2$stand a bully and $_3$defend a victim who $_4$is being attacked.
                                                                            [   ]

B. Choose the word or phrase that best completes the sentence.

3. People who use social media are usually pleased when they get approval but they don't like to be . . .
   a. put back   b. put down   c. put off   d. put over

4. When you pull out of a competition or a business deal you . . . from it.
   a. escape   b. remove   c. take off   d. withdraw

5. In the evening, the restaurant . . . tables and chairs so that customers could sit outside and watch the sunset.
   a. brought up   b. got over   c. set up   d. watched over

❄ Listening Challenge ❄

Listen and fill in the missing words.

1. Sharing ¹[   ] with friends and acquaintances is ²[
   ] of true friendship, so we ³[   ] it is accurate.

2. One sign of ¹[   ] is a willingness to ²[   ]
   you when someone says bad things about you, ³[   ] you are
   present.

3. When the gates of the stadium ¹[   ], there was ²[
   ] heading toward the stalls trying to ³[   ] T-shirts that
   commemorated the game.

4. When John ¹[   ], he didn't like to eat unusual foods, but when
   he became an adult, he ²[   ] anything that was served to him in
   ³[   ].

5. My dog has ¹[   ] when he encounters a strange dog that is
   ²[   ], but when he encounters a cat, I have to ³[
   ] from running away.

Going Further (for discussion or research)

1. Have there been other cases in which "freedom of speech" in Japan has been
   abused?

2. Is it possible to distinguish between accurate information and misinformation
   (disinformation)? If so, how can you do it?

Position of the Self Defense Force in Japan

画像は 2022 年の中露合同軍事演習の模様。ロシアによるウクライナ侵攻は軍事大国の横暴さと恐ろしさをまざまざと見せつけることになった。北朝鮮はことあるごとに日本近海にミサイルを撃ち込んでその軍事力を誇示している。東シナ海の尖閣諸島をめぐる日本と中国との緊張関係は相変わらず続いたままだ。台湾と中国との関係も一触即発の危機をはらんでいる。日本の自衛隊は建前上は正式な軍隊ではないが、実際には立派な軍隊であるし、軍事予算は増える一方で、憲法改正を支持する国民も増えている。はたして、日本の置かれている国際環境の中で自国の平和を守るためには何が必要なのだろうか。

Position of the Self Defense Force in Japan

21

Following World War II, the Occupation administration—known in Japan as GHQ—initially set out to demilitarize Japan. The country was prohibited from possessing any military force at all. When the Korean War broke out, however, the Occupation changed its policies in order to allow Japan to establish a national self-defense organization. The awkward arrangement that led to the peace treaty and the return of sovereignty to Japan held that Japan would not maintain an army but would be protected by American military forces on bases in Japan. 5

Japan has an army in all but name. What it maintains is the Self Defense Force (SDF). Its focus is on defense, such as hunting submarines, warding off warplanes, patrolling its EEZs, and keeping an eye on missile launches potentially flying over Japan. All offensive duties are left to American troops stationed in Japan, if such duties should be required. 10

Until now, Japan has maintained a self-imposed restriction on defense spending that is less than 1% of the national GDP. The most obvious new offensive capabilities include the upgrade of the *Izumo*, Japan's largest warship. The SDF has downplayed this as "an escort ship." But with a deck full of F-35 jets, it would be hard not to see what it really is: an aircraft-carrier. Another upgrade is the acquisition of long-range missiles that can be fired from a warplane. These might serve as a deterrent, given that Japanese warplanes scramble against Chinese incursions several hundred times a year. 15

20

● NOTES ●

1 **the Occupation administration**「占領統治」／2 **GHQ** = General Headquarters「連合国軍最高司令官総司令部」／2 **demilitarize**「非軍事化する」de- 分離・否定の意、militarize「軍事化する」／2 **prohibit ~ from …**「〜が…することを禁じる」／3 **the Korean War**「朝鮮戦争」。1948 年に韓国と北朝鮮のあいだで生じ、1953 年に休戦したまま現在に至る。／4 **allow ~ to …**「〜が…することを可能にする」／5- **The awkward arrangement …**　この文章は関係代名詞と接続詞の that に注意。また not ~ but …「〜でなく…」／5 **the peace treaty**「平和条約」／6 **sovereignty**「主権」／7 **base**「基地」／8 **in all but name**「事実上」／8 **What it maintains …**　文頭の what は先行詞を含む関係代名詞。ここでは目的格。／8 **the Self Defense Force**「自衛隊」／9 **ward off**「を追い払う」／10 **EEZ** = Exclusive Economic Zone「排他的経済水域」／10 **keep an eye on**「を見張る」／11 **troop**「軍隊」／13 **self-imposed**「自主的な」／13 **restriction**「制限」／14 **GDP** = Gross Domestic Product「国内総生産」／15 **downplay**「過少申告する」／16 **escort ship**「護衛艦」／17 **aircraft-carrier**「航空母艦」／17 **acquisition**「搭載」／18 **deterrent**「抑止力」／18 **given**「を考えると」／19 **scramble**「緊急発進する」／19 **incursion**「侵入」

✳ *Comprehension Check* ✳

1. The demilitarization of Japan . . .

    a. was fully carried out.

    b. began under the Occupation administration.

    c. prevented Japan from having any military forces.

2. The main duties of the SDF can be described as . . .

    a. defensive actions.

    b. offensive actions.

    c. upgraded actions.

    An immediate issue for Japan is dealing with frequent Chinese incursions into waters around the Senkaku Islands in the East China Sea. China claims them and calls them Diaoyu, but Japan controls them. The concerns grew larger in 2021 and 2022 with China's new Coast Guard Law, by which China seems to be intruding in what Japan contends are its territorial waters. China claims it is conducting what it 5 calls law enforcement activities. The new law gives the Coast Guard the right to use weapons when national sovereignty is being infringed on by foreign organizations and individuals at sea. This is not in accord with international law or with Japan's Coast Guard Law. If the Chinese Coast Guard develops into China's second navy, there is no way that the Japan's Coast Guard can go beyond its role and take military 10 action.

    Although the South China Sea is not a direct threat to Japan, China's building and occupation of airstrips, radar systems, and missile sites on artificial islands constructed on reefs there also pose a potential problem. They make China's naval reach longer, perhaps long enough to put pressure on Japan. The greatest concern is 15 China's claims that Taiwan is part of China. The world has seen how the "one country two systems" policy worked in Hong Kong. Now there is concern that Taiwan could be next in line.

● NOTES ●

2 **waters**「海域」複数形であることに注意。／ 2 **the East China Sea**「東シナ海」／ 3 **Diaoyu**「釣魚島」尖閣諸島にある魚釣島に対する中国での呼称。／ 4 **Coast Guard Law**「海上警備隊法」中国の Coast Guard は「中国海警局」で、それに関する法律は「中国海警法」。日本の Coast Guard は「海上保安庁」で、それに関する法律は「海上保安庁法」。／ 5 **what Japan contends are ...** what は先行詞を含む関係代名詞。ここでは目的格。次文の what も同様。／ 6 **enforcement**「執行」／ 7 **is being infringed on** 受動態が現在進行形にな

っていることに注意。infringe on「を侵害する」／ 8 **in accord with**「と一致する」／ 10 **there is no way that**「that 以下を行なうわけにはゆかない」／ 11 **Although the South China Sea is …** Although を接続詞とする複文。主節の主語が並列で長くなっているので注意。／ 13 **airstrip**「滑走路」／ 14 **reef**「岩礁」／ 14 **pose**「を提出する」／ 14 **naval**「海軍の」。cf. navy「海軍」／ 16 **one country two systems**「一国二制度」／ 18 **next in line** ここでの line は「列」のこと。

✳*Comprehension Check* ✳

3. The phrase "there is no way" means . . .
   a. it is infringement.
   b. it is immediate.
   c. it is impossible.

4. The most serious potential threat to Japan is . . .
   a. China's artificial islands.
   b. China's claims regarding Taiwan.
   c. China's naval power.

🎧
23
    One issue that repeatedly surfaces is how Japan might actually protect itself. While Japanese seem to feel the need to be less dependent on American bases and feel that Okinawans bear an excessive burden, they are unable to agree to an alternative. Given North Korea's repeated launching of missiles over Japanese airspace or into the seas near Japan without prior notice, there is reason to be concerned. Scrambling 5 SDF jets to challenge jets from an intruding country is one thing, but stopping a supersonic missile is entirely different.

    At the very least, Japan should have an advanced warning system. But when the government proposed establishing an Aegis Ashore facility in Akita Prefecture, the local governments opposed the idea. It seemed like a textbook case of NIMBY: not 10 in my back yard. In other words, Japan needs such facilities, but local people don't want it in their prefecture.

    If Japanese have fallen into a condition of *heiwa boke*, then it may be time to wake up.

● NOTES ●
1 **surface**「浮上する」ここでは自動詞。／ 3 **Okinawan**「沖縄県民」／ 3 **excessive**「過度の」／ 5 **prior notice**「事前通告」／ 6 **challenge**「に抗議する」／ 6 **intrude**「侵入する」／ 6 **~ is one thing, but … is different.**「～と…はわけが違う」／ 7 **supersonic**「超音速の」／ 8 **At the very least**「せめて、最低でも」cf.

at least「少なくとも」／9 **Aegis Ashore facility**「イージス・アショア設備」弾道ミサイル迎撃システムの名前で、イージスは艦船に搭載されるが、イージス・アショアは陸上に設置される。cf. ashore「陸上の」／10 **local government**「地元自治体」／11 **in other words**「言い換えれば」

✽*Comprehension Check*✽

5. In regard to how Japan could realistically protect itself, . . .
   a. there are many potential alternatives to American bases.
   b. an advanced warning system would be more than sufficient.
   c. few options have been agreed on so far.

❊ **Structure Practice** ❊

A. Choose the one underlined word or phrase that should be corrected or rewritten. Then change it so that the sentence is correct.

1. After World War II, the ₁debate over whether Japan ₂had been allowed to possess an army and navy was finally ₃settled by permitting the country to have forces ₄that performed defensive duties.   [   ]

2. While most Japanese believe that Okinawa ₁endures special hardships due to the American bases there, they seem ₂unable to find a ₃suitable alternative that local communities would ₄agree.   [   ]

B. Choose the word or phrase that best completes the sentence.

3. I'm afraid that I will not be able to attend the convention because I have a(n) . . . engagement.
   a. advanced   b. earlier   c. following   d. prior

4. In areas where roads may be flooded or covered with debris, drones can . . . cars and trucks as methods of delivering emergency food and supplies following a disaster.
   a. change   b. exchange   c. replace   d. substitute

5. Ships and planes that patrol national borders may . . . foreign countries from entering the area without permission.

    a. deter   b. deterrent   c. put off   d. put out

❄ Listening Challenge ❄

🎧 Listen and fill in the missing words.
24

1. One of ¹[   ] researching and discussing the events of ²[   ] is to learn how similar events ³[   ] in the future.

2. Occasionally the ¹[   ] dependency surfaces ²[   ] but there seems to be ³[   ] to make Japan more self-sufficient.

3. When ¹[   ] the CEO from New York ²[   ] Tokyo this Friday, we ³[   ] to make preparations for a party.

4. For ¹[   ] I have maintained ²[   ] routine of daily exercise, ³[   ] early, and eating healthy food.

5. There is ¹[   ] regarding how Japan ²[   ] its EEZ against possible infringement ³[   ].

Going Further (for discussion or research)

1. Why does Japan have a Self Defense Force and not a military?

2. If Japan had an army and navy, should military duty be required of all citizens of the country?

CHAPTER **7** 原発依存

Should Nuclear Power Dependency Be Halted?

地球温暖化に対する危機感に伴う自然エネルギーへの転換が思うようにいかないなかで「原発再稼働」が言われるようになった。また、ウクライナ侵攻に伴う経済制裁に対してロシアが対抗手段としてとった天然ガスの輸出を一部遮断する措置は、ロシアが最大のエネルギー供給源であるヨーロッパの国々に大きな打撃を与えた。日本もロシアとの極東の共同資源プロジェクト「サハリン2」の先行きが不安になり、原発廃止の世論に水を差すような事態になった。はたして、核廃棄物や安全性の問題を十分に考慮した上で、温室効果ガスの排出量が少ないという原子力発電の「利点」は議論されているのだろうか。

Should Nuclear Power Dependency Be Halted?

25

Japan is entirely dependent upon imports of different forms of fuel to power its factories, businesses, and transportation and heat and light its housing. Wind, solar, thermal, and wave power are steadily increasing but are still insignificant. LNG, natural gas, and petroleum have to be imported from distant sources. Therefore, the appeal of nuclear power is hard to resist. 5

In June 2021, Kansai Electric Power Company (KEPCO) rebooted its No. 3 reactor in the Mihama nuclear station in Fukui Prefecture. Osaka and its industries need power, said the company and local businesses. But the logic of the decision to restart the reactor was hard to grasp.

First of all, the standard approved lifetime of a nuclear reactor in Japan was once 10 set at 40 years. But now Japan is considering extending the maximum service period beyond 60 years due to the anticipated public opposition to construction of any new plants. The ruling Liberal Democratic Party and some business circles contended that extending the use of current plants is easier than building new ones. The public, however, showed concerns about the safety of aging reactors, especially those that 15 have previously had accidents.

● NOTES ●

1 **power**「に動力を与える」ここでは他動詞。／3 **thermal**「熱の」ここでは火力発電を指す。／3 **insignificant**「軽微な」。in- 否定の意、significant「重要な」／3 **LNG** = Liquefied Natural Gas「液化天然ガス」／4 **petroleum** = coal oil ／6 **Kansai Electric Power Company**「関西電力」／6 **reboot**「を再稼働する」／7 **reactor**「原子炉」／7 **the Mihama nuclear station**「美浜原子力発電所」／7 **Osaka and its industries need power, …** 倒置文であり、文頭からカンマまでが say の目的語。／13 **ruling**「与党の」cf. rule「支配する」／13 **Liberal Democratic Party**「自民党」／13 **business circle**「業界」／15 **aging**「老朽化した」

✱ Comprehension Check ✱

1. Electric power generated by renewable sources such as solar and wave power . . .
    a. remains less important.
    b. contributes significantly.
    c. can be imported.

2. Extending the service period of nuclear reactors . . .
    a. prevents the adoption of thermal and wind generated power.
    b. has been guaranteed to be a safe for the local communities.
    c. is seen by some parties as a solution that is simpler than building new ones.

🎧
26
    Fukui No. 3 was restarted in its 44th year by special approval from the governing agency. Given the poor record of failings in regulation and oversight, one could hardly be confident that this restart would be safe, even in a "younger" reactor. Had KEPCO learned much from the Tokyo Electric Power Company (TEPCO) disaster in Fukushima, where an earthquake and tsunami knocked out the Fukushima No. 1 5
nuclear station?

    Further, there was a lack of transparency about how permission was given for the old reactor. It was clear, however, that subsidies were provided to sweeten local opinion in order to get the reboot approval. In fact, a subsidy of ¥2.5 billion to local communities was agreed upon before the governor of Fukui prefecture agreed to the 10
restart.

    Despite the issues of the Fukushima disaster and the restart of the aged Fukui facility, the issue of energy security looms large. Until the Fukushima disaster, some 30% of Japan's power came from nuclear plants. That figure is now roughly 6%. To make up for this shortage, more fuel must be brought from overseas. Both the 15
transportation of the fuel and the burning of it produce carbon dioxide, and Japan has promised to lower emissions 26% from 2013 levels by 2030 under its commitments to the Paris Accord.

    Nuclear power is hard for a resource-limited nation like Japan to surrender. It produces carbon-free power nonstop. It requires very little fuel imports from overseas. 20
It takes up little land, in contrast with onshore wind turbines and solar energy farms. But some 39% of Japanese people want to see all nuclear plants closed. With the Russian invasion of Ukraine, the story became more complex. Every source of fuel seemed endangered, including fuel imported directly from Russia.

●NOTES●

1 **Fukui No. 3** 美浜原発の原子炉 3 号機を指す。／2 **oversight**「監督」／2 **one can hardly be ...** one は一般的に人を指す。hardly「ほとんど〜ない」／4 **the Tokyo Electric Power Company**「東京電力」／5 **where** 関係副詞。／5 **the Fukushima No. 1 nuclear station**「福島第一原子力発電所」。2011 年の東日本大震災で事故が起こり、放射能汚染が広範囲に生じた。／7 **transparency**「透明性」／8 **It was clear that ...** 文頭の it は仮主語で that 以下を指す。／8 **subsidy**「助成金」／8 **sweeten**「機嫌をとる」。cf. sweet「甘い、優しい」／10 **agree upon**「申し合わせる」／10 **governor**「知事」／13 **loom large**「立ちはだかる」。cf. loom「(危険などが) 迫る」／15 **make up for**「を埋め合わせる」／16 **carbon dioxide**「二酸化炭素」／17 **commitment**「公約」／18 **the Paris Accord**「パリ協定」。2015 年に行なわれた国連気候変動枠組条約締約国会議で合意された、気候変動問題に関する取り決め。／20 **carbon**「炭素」／20 **nonstop**「休憩なしに」／21 **take up**「を必要とする」／21 **in contrast with**「と対照的に」／21 **onshore**「沿岸の」／23 **invasion**「侵攻」

✳ *Comprehension Check* ✳

3. In order to encourage approval from local people and governments . . .

    a. little attention was given to the events at Fukushima No. 1.

    b. Kepco offered subsidies to the community.

    c. new regulations and oversight were put into place.

4. Due to Japan's commitment to the Paris Accord . . .

    a. the country needs to reduce its dependence on solar power.

    b. it prefers to shift to thermal and wave power.

    c. imports and burning of fuels should be reduced.

27

     One subject that is rarely raised in the discussions of nuclear power is how to deal with nuclear waste. Finland is at the forefront in dealing with such waste. Its Onkalo—"cavity" or "pit" in Finnish—will be the first permanent disposal site for high-level nuclear waste. The key words here are "high-level nuclear waste" and "permanent disposal site." By permanent, the Finns mean 100,000 years. This amazing   5 project offers hope for the future of nuclear power, after hopes were diminished by the Chernobyl and Fukushima Daiichi disasters.

     Being a land of volcanoes, regular earthquakes, and tsunamis, Japan has no place to put its waste. The nuclear waste that has been gathered from the Fukushima Daiichi site is still accumulating in "temporary storage" and there is little hope of finding a   10 permanent location for any of it. Release of contaminated water into the Pacific is resisted by local fishermen, nearby residents, and other Asian nations.

     If Japan cannot find a dependable way of permanently storing nuclear waste, is it legitimate to continue creating more nuclear waste?

●NOTES●

1 **One subject that …** 主語が関係代名詞節で後置修飾されているのに注意。／2 **nuclear waste**「核廃棄物」／2 **at the forefront**「先頭に」／3 **Onkalo**「オンカロ」／3 **cavity** = pit「空洞」／3 **Finnish**「フィンランド語」。cf. Finns「フィンランド人」／3 **permanent disposal site**「最終処分場」／5 **By permanent**「〈永久的な〉の語で」 cf. permanent「永久的な」、permanently「永久に」／7 **Chernobyl**「チェルノブイリ」1986年、当地の原発で事故が起こり、放射能汚染が広範囲に生じた。／11 **contaminated**「汚染された」／11 **the Pacific**「太平洋」／13 **dependable**「信頼できる」／14 **legitimate**「合理的な、適法な、正当な」

✳ *Comprehension Check* ✳

5. Imitating the example of Finland's Onkalo site . . .

   a. would be a good means of temporary storage of nuclear waste.

   b. is hardly possible in Japan due to its geological features.

   c. raises hopes for a successfully dealing with waste from nuclear reactors.

❈ Structure Practice ❈

A. Choose the one underlined word or phrase that should be corrected or rewritten. Then change it so that the sentence is correct.

1. The ₁original date ₂set on the industrial exhibition was May 12, but the event had to be ₃pushed back one week ₄due to logistical problems.   [   ]

2. Considering the ₁significant increase in the price of ₂imported oil, ₃switching to alternate sources of power has much more ₄appealing.   [   ]

B. Choose the word or phrase that best completes the sentence.

3. Because we were late in getting started on our journey, we will have to . . . it by taking only a short break for lunch along the way.

   a. account for   b. make up for   c. provide for   d. reach for

4. I was carrying a big box into the living room and couldn't see where I was going, so I clumsily knocked . . . the chair.

   a. at   b. off   c. on   d. over

5. Ellen is enthusiastically searching for a job and has . . . of finding a job where she could make better use of her experience with wind turbines.

   a. hopeful   b. hopefulness   c. high hopes   d. hopelessness

❋ Listening Challenge ❋

🎧 **Listen and fill in the missing words.**

1. After his ¹[   ] to set up a new company, it is ²[   ]
   to grasp why he is trying to do it again ³[   ].

2. It is ¹[   ] that some politicians and businesspeople still believe
   ²[   ] is not the cause of ³[   ] the Earth.

3. Todd's ¹[   ] at the private school ²[   ] the
   beginning of September ³[   ] May.

4. Wind turbines ¹[   ] in shallow water offshore ²[   ], although the ³[   ] is somewhat easier.

5. Recently workers ¹[   ] the attempts of their employers ²[   ] to return to the office ³[   ].

Going Further (for discussion or research)

1. For Japan, are there realistic energy alternatives that could replace nuclear power?

2. What lessons has Japan learned from the Fukushima nuclear power plant disaster?

CHAPTER *8* 少子化対策

Fertility Decline and Initiatives

少子化に歯止めがかからない。日本の総人口はこのままでいくと 2065 年には 8,808 万
人になるものと推計される（国立社会保障・人口問題研究所、2017 年）。2100 年には
6000 万人程度になると予測する向きもある。少子化の要因として、非婚化・晩婚化及び
女性の出生率低下などがあげられ、国による対策が打ち出されても、事態は一向に改善さ
れない。人口減少が進む社会的要因にはいくつかの問題が絡まっていて、その解決策を講
じるのは容易なことではない。私たちは、まず人口減少の厳しい現実を直視し、その上で、
「人口減少社会を明るい未来にするべき」議論を始める必要があるのではないだろうか。

Fertility Decline and Initiatives

🎧 29

The media regularly takes up the issue of the declining population of Japan and how to solve *the issue*. Actually, it is more complex than that. There are several overlapping issues.

For one thing, companies have cut back on the number of regular employees on their staffs. They have turned to contract workers, part-timers, and gig workers to 5 do jobs that were formerly done by full-time employees. The latter would at least seem to have long-term guarantees of income, company-paid health insurance, and a fairly stable schedule. The former group has no such guarantees. They work for a certain length of time, without insurance, and when that job is done, they have to look for another source of income. They are constantly looking for work. For them, it is 10 virtually impossible to plan for the future.

Such non-regular workers may be able to cover their basic daily expenses, but they have little in savings for an emergency. And buying housing and starting a family are beyond imagination.

In June 2022, the Japanese government published the findings of a survey on 15 gender equality. The paper also dealt with the issue of marriage. It found that the number of marriages had dropped over the past year to roughly 514,000. To put that into perspective, this figure is the lowest since the end of World War II.

●NOTES●

3 **overlapping**「重なっている」／4 **cut back on**「を削減する」／4 **regular employee** = full-time employee「正社員」／5 **contract worker**「契約社員」／5 **gig worker**「ギグ・ワーカー」短期的に単発で仕事を受注する労働形態を指す。cf. free lance「自営業者」／7 **health insurance**「健康保険」／11 **virtually**「事実上」／12 **cover**「（費用）をまかなう」／13 **saving**「貯蓄」／15 **survey**「調査」／16 **gender equality**「男女共同参画」／17 **put into perspective**「を大局的に見る」。ここでは歴史的な視野で見ることを指す。

✳Comprehension Check✳

1. Those who are not regular company employees . . .

   a. are not as fortunate as contract workers.

   b. do have health insurance paid by the company.

   c. must regularly search for new jobs.

2. Workers who are not regular employees . . .

   a. are prohibited from having families.

   b. will hesitate to marry and have children.

   c. do not have money for basic expenses.

In the survey, of single Japanese in their 30s who have never been married, roughly a quarter of both men and women preferred to remain single. Getting married, to them, meant losing freedom. More than the women, the men who responded gave financial concerns and job insecurity as reasons for avoiding marriage. More than the men, the women who responded wanted to avoid housework burdens, child care, and nursing care that usually came with marriage. The media even adopted a new   5 term, *ohitorisama*, to refer to a new life style and a new market, designed for working singles who are comfortable with remaining single.

The Japanese government consistently expresses concerns about the declining population, but is unwilling to significantly open the doors to migrants from oversees. To most politicians, the desirable way of increasing workers is to put more Japanese   10 women in the workplace. But for all the talk the government does about gender equality in the workplace, it overlooks two major obstacles.

●NOTES●

4 **insecurity**「不安定さ」。in- 否定の意、security「安全、安定」／6 **nursing care**「介護」。cf. nurse「を看病する、を子守する、を介護する」／10 **unwilling**「好まない、気が進まない」。un- 否定の意、willing「自発的な」／10 **significantly**「大々的に」／10 **migrant**「移住者」／11 **desirable**「望ましい」／12 **But for all the talk about**「の話ばかりする割には」／13 **overlook**「を見落とす、見過ごす」。overlook は「を見渡す、見下ろす」も意味するので注意。cf. oversee「（仕事・労働者）を監督する」

✳ *Comprehension Check* ✳

3. A major reason single women give for not wishing to get married is . . .

   a. a desire to avoid housework and carrying for family members.

   b. financial worries and concerns about job security.

   c. a dislike of remaining single and keeping a regular job.

One is the harassment of women who get married and those who get pregnant. Companies take it for granted that these women will voluntarily resign their jobs. Another is the long waiting lines for day care for children. Publicly-subsidized day care slots are limited. Families have a hard time finding preschools for 3 to 5 year olds close enough to their workplaces. To meet the need, the government needs to ⁵ provide more funding on subsidized slots, hire more teachers, and guarantee higher wages to the teachers.

Parents who cannot find public funded day care are forced to search for private, unsubsidized facilities. But these facilities cost much more and are not required to meet government standards for the number of licensed teachers. In some cases, the ¹⁰ teachers may not be sufficiently trained or even licensed.

And what about women who want to return to the workplace after their children are old enough to go to school? Are companies going to welcome them with open arms when they return? Or are they going to push these women into minor positions? If the government is serious about increasing the population, then it must enforce ¹⁵ equal treatment for women even in private companies.

There is, however, one different way of looking at population decline: it could be a good thing. The cities could be less crowded. The government could concentrate its services in limited areas. People would be less stressed from rush hour commutes. Life could slow down a bit. Is it really necessary to increase the population? Maybe ²⁰ not.

●NOTES●

1 **the harassment of women** ここでは「女性を対象とする、あるいは女性についてのハラスメント」を指す。／ 2 **take it for granted** 「を当たり前だと思う」／ 2 **voluntarily** 「自発的に」cf. volunteer「志願者、義勇兵」／ 3 **day care for children** 「託児施設」／ 3 **subsidize** 「補助する」／ 4 **slot** 「枠」／ 4 **preschool** 「保育園、幼稚園」／ 5 **close to** 「に近い」／ 5 **meet** 「（需要・要件など）を満たす」／ 6 **funding** 「基金」／ 10 **license** 「を認可する」。ここでは他動詞。／ 13 **with open arms** 歓迎の意を示す。／ 14 **minor position** ここでは仕事上の役割を指す。／ 15 **enforce** 「を強要する」／ 16 **private company** 「民間企業」／ 19 **stress** 「を緊張させる」ここでは他動詞。／ 19 **commute** 「通勤」

✳ Comprehension Check ✳

4. Parents with young children would probably prefer . . .

   a. private day care services for their children.

   b. subsidized public day care services.

   c. to live with their parents to help with child care.

5. According to the article, companies and government offices should . . .

   a. avoid placing women in the same positions as men.

   b. place women in minor positions when they return from maternity leave.

   c. guarantee gender equality in the workplace.

❀ Structure Practice ❀

A. Choose the one underlined word or phrase that should be corrected or rewritten. Then change it so that the sentence is correct.

1. Contract workers and other ₁<u>non-regular</u> employees face a number of ₂<u>struggles</u>, ₃<u>include</u> the need to ₄<u>continue</u> searching for work.   [   ]

2. ₁<u>Enforce</u> the equal treatment of men and women in the ₂<u>workplace</u> does not seem ₃<u>to be high</u> on ₄<u>the agenda of</u> the national government.   [   ]

B. Choose the word or phrase that best completes the sentence.

3. We get along well together because our interests and beliefs . . . .
   a. overachieve   b. overlap   c. overlook   d. oversight

4. Because he had . . . experience with public funding of day care facilities, he was put in charge of surveying the current status of the local needs.
   a. insufficient   b. subsidized   c. sufficient   d. unsubsidized

5. When you judge the real importance of something by considering its relation to everything else you . . . .
   a. depend on your own experience   b. judge it by your beliefs
   c. put it in perspective   d. take it out of perspective

❄ Listening Challenge ❄

🎧 32 **Listen and fill in the missing words.**

1. ¹[   ] reduce overtime work, ²[   ] recognize
    that they need to ³[   ].

2. Enforcing ¹[   ] for women and men ²[   ]
    is important for private companies ³[   ] government offices.

3. Allowing ¹[   ] to decline somewhat ²[   ] a
    bad thing, because it might ³[   ] in large metropolitan
    areas.

4. Several varieties of harassment ¹[   ], such as abusive language
    and discriminatory behavior ²[   ] gender or ethnic origin, can be
    highly stressful when the ³[   ] needs to keep the job to earn a
    living.

5. For people with free time and ¹[   ], a gig job is a way to earn
    a bit of cash, but people ²[   ] gig jobs to earn their living, it is
    ³[   ] of employment.

Going Further (for discussion or research)

1. What aspects of Japanese daily life would need to change in order to encourage
    more couples to have more children?

2. Is the concept of *ohitorisama* a positive, or does it have a downside?

CHAPTER **9** デジタル化と行政

Digitization and
Public Administration

2021年9月にデジタル庁が発足した。それに先だつ6月には、政府は民間企業や官民の取引の契約書で押印は必ずしも必要ではないとの見解を示した。押印という典型的なアナログ行為を廃止したのは、普及に躍起となっているマイナンバーカードを始めとした行政のデジタル化の推進を目指す政府にとって、国民に対する大きなアピールとなった。行政のデジタル化のメリットは、業務の効率化、紙資源の節約、勤務時間外でのサービスの充実など様ざまなことが期待される。しかし、ITに疎く周りに頼れる者もいない高齢者が置き去りにされないためにはどうすれば良いのか、対策は検討されているのだろうか。

Digitization and Public Administration

33

Visitors from around the world come to Akihabara to view the latest technological miracles in consumer goods. But there are limits to how such technology has been put to work inside Japan itself. Japan has some of the world's best mobile and broadband networks, yet its government agencies seem unable to escape from paper documents and authorizing services with a *hanko*. Then-minister for administrative reform Kono 5 Taro estimated at the beginning of his time in that position that in some 15,000 cases, a traditional personal seal was required to carry out a bureaucratic procedure. That has since been significantly reduced.

According to an article in *The Economist* in early 2021 entertainingly titled "Update required," in a survey of 30 countries in the OECD, Japan came in last place 10 in terms of the percentage of the digital services that the government provides. In 2018, in Iceland, the top runner, 80% of its citizens requested something from the government online. In that year in Japan, only 7.3% of its citizens used online services for that purpose. In addition, Japan seems attached to using antiquated fax machines, rarely updating many public information websites, and requiring personal visits to 15 offices to carry out applications.

●NOTES●

title **digitization**「デジタル化」／ 2 **put to work**「を働かせる、に仕事をさせる」／ 5 **authorize**「を認証する」／ 5 **then-**「当時の」／ 5 **minister for administrative reform**「行政刷新担当大臣」cf. minister「大臣」、administrative「行政上の」／ 7 **personal seal**「認め印」cf. registered seal「実印」／ 7 **bureaucratic**「役所の」／ 9 ***The Economist*** イギリスの週刊誌『エコノミスト』／ 9 **entertainingly**「愉快に」／ 10 **OECD** = Organization for Economic Cooperation and Development「経済協力開発機構」／ 11 **in terms of**「に関して」／ 14 **attach to**「に執着がある」／ 14 **antiquated**「時代遅れの」／ 15 **rarely**「めったに〜しない」／ 15 **personal** ここでは「当人の」／ 16 **application**「申請」

✳*Comprehension Check*✳

1. Japan's advanced technology . . .

    a. has not been fully adopted within government agencies.

    b. is rapidly reducing the need for documents and personal seals.

    c. has drawn foreign companies to set up operations in Japan.

2. It is not true that . . .

    a. digital administrative services in Iceland are advanced.

    b. public information on government websites is updated regularly.

    c. visits to Japanese government offices are necessary for applications.

It is estimated that there are some 56,000 administrative procedures that are carried out by the national government. As of 2019, however, only 7.5% could be completed online. It would seem that the new ministry of digital reform has a lot of work to do. Members of the media and the public at large have suggested that Japan needs its own version of Taiwan's popular digital minister, Audrey Tang, who rapidly 5 enabled Taiwan to deal with something simple like obtaining masks to prevent the spread of Covid-19.

The pandemic has made the need for rapid digitization clear to the government and the public as well. While some nations managed to send out cash relief to families and businesses within weeks, Japan's payments took months and often required 10 multiple visits to government offices to submit multiple handwritten forms just to apply for payments.

Changing this will not be easy. At the national level, each ministry and agency has its own "digital architecture." Below this, each local government has its own version. It will take time for these entities to develop compatible systems that make sharing 15 data possible. There will also be resistance from the elderly, who will not have the devices or the skills required for carrying out procedures online.

● NOTES ●

1 **It is estimated that …** 文頭の it は仮主語で that 以下を指す。／2 **as of**「現在」／3 **the new ministry of digital reform**「新設のデジタル改革担当省」日本には 2020 年から 21 年まで、デジタル庁 (Digital Agency) を設置する準備としてデジタル改革担当大臣が置かれていた。cf. ministry「省」、agency「庁」／4 **public at large**「一般大衆」cf. at large「全体として」／6 **enable ~ to …**「～が…することを可能にする」／7 **Covid-19** 2019 年 12 月に初の感染例が確認され、世界的な大流行を引き起こした新型コロナウイルス感染症。／9 **cash relief**「現金給付」cf. relief「救援物資、基金」／10 **require ~ to …**「～が…することを要求する」／11 **handwritten**「手書きの」／14 **architecture**「建築、構成」／15 **it takes time for ~ to …**「～が…するには時間がかかる」文頭の it は仮主語。／15 **entity**「自治体」独立した存在一般を示す。／15 **compatible**「互換性のある」／17 **required** 以下は the devices or the skills を後置修飾する形容詞句。

✳ *Comprehension Check* ✳

3. According to the passage, reforming administrative procedures in Japan . . .

   a. has not been attempted until now.

   b. would require quite a lot of funding.

   c. will require a lot of effort.

4. Distributing cash relief to families and businesses . . .
    a. required submitting documents to government offices in person.
    b. was implemented by new forms of digital architecture.
    c. made use of compatible government agency systems.

35

    Bringing about change may require that bureaucrats at local government office counters become digital-assistance workers who are competent in helping older citizens without their own digital devices apply for services. That this is essential was made clear during the vaccination registration process. Finding vaccination sites with available slots was hard enough for digitally savvy residents with devices at home. 5 Older residents with neither the devices nor the skills to do anything online had to do what they had always done: call dozens of times until someone answered the phone, or go to the municipal office and ask for assistance.

    The benefits of digitization are clear. It saves time, reduces the consumption of paper, allows people to apply for or receive documents outside of regular 9-to-5 work 10 hours, and increases productivity. But it will require a considerable adjustment in how Japan's government operates.

    And it will require the young generations to help their elderly neighbors and family members. It is hard enough for the persistent to navigate simple websites. One can hardly expect someone who can barely use a smartphone to fill in government 15 forms on a website, make train reservations on a JR site, or check a QR code for a hazard map of the local neighborhood.

● NOTES ●

1 **bring about**「をもたらす」／1 **bureaucrat**「官僚、公務員」／2 **competent**「能力がある」／3 **That this is essential ...** 文頭の That は名詞節を導く。／4 **vaccination**「ワクチン接種」cf. vaccinate「ワクチン接種をする」／5 **slot**「枠」／5 **savvy**「よく知っている」／7 **what they had always done** what は先行詞を含む関係代名詞。ここでは目的格。／8 **municipal**「地方自治体の」／14 **persistent**「根気強いひと」。形容詞だが、ここでは名詞扱い。／15 **hardly**「ほとんど〜しない」／15 **expect 〜 to ...**「〜が…することを期待する」ここでは目的語 someone の後ろに関係代名詞節が挟まっているので注意。／15 **barely**「かろうじて〜する」／16 **JR** = Japan Railways ／16 **QR code** 縦横の2方向に情報が配置されたバーコードを指す。「QR コード」は日本語で、英語では 2D (two-dimensional) barcode。

✳Comprehension Check✳

5. Digitization of procedures in Japanese municipal offices . . .

    a. does not require that every citizen have digital devices.

    b. will require office workers to help older citizens.

    c. would probably decrease the productivity of government offices.

❄ Structure Practice ❄

A. Choose the one underlined word or phrase that should be corrected or rewritten. Then change it so that the sentence is correct.

1. ₁Despite one would expect Japan, a leader in technology, to ₂apply its achieved skills in the government agencies, it seems that there is a significant ₃lag time between ₄creation and implementation.   [   ]

2. Elderly citizens are ₁likely to have difficulty in ₂figuring how to access information and complete application forms online, ₃especially if they are not skilled in using a smartphone and do not ₄own a laptop.   [   ]

B. Choose the word that best completes the sentence.

3. The government often requires several separate documents to carry . . . procedures for applying for public relief.

    a. on   b. onto   c. out   d. over

4. After returning to my job following a three-day weekend, I found it time-consuming to . . . to all of the emails in my inbox.

    a. apply   b. contain   c. obtain   d. reply

5. It takes considerable persistence to . . . about effective reforms when the bureaucracy is so dependent on non-digitized processes.

    a. ask   b. bring   c. discuss   d. promote

❊ Listening Challenge ❊

🎧 36 **Listen and fill in the missing words.**

1. The ¹[   ] typewriters to computers was ²[
    ] by the use of the same keyboard, but all of the new functions ³[
        ] to get used to.

2. Being able ¹[   ] outside of local government office hours at
    a convenience store has ²[   ] for people who can't get to
    city hall or a bank ³[   ] work week.

3. My father ¹[   ] that he was not going to help me financially
    ²[   ] from high school, so I ³[   ] scholarships
    and loans through the university.

4. Obtaining ¹[   ] from dependable sources about vaccinations
    and ²[   ] is important, because social media communicates
    a lot of misinformation ³[   ] who just want to have
    followers.

5. It is ¹[   ] when government websites are not updated, ²[
        ] that are no longer active, and ³[   ] in fees and
    procedures.

Going Further (for discussion or research)

1. There seems to be a generation gap in terms of use of digital services between
   young people and the elderly. How might that gap be bridged?

2. How secure is personal data in smartphones, bank cards, and websites?

Covid Measures and
National Character

「想定外の問題」にぶつかった時に人はどう対応するのか？　個人の場合は取り乱して暫らく茫然とするのも許されるのかもしれない。しかし、国民や住民の命と安全を守るのが第一の使命である政府や自治体の長にはそうした甘えは禁物だ。COVID-19 のパンデミックでは日本の行政の問題点が露呈した。国と地方自治体の長との間にはこれまで経験をしたことのない事態に対する対処をめぐって議論が交わされはしたが、国が強力なイニシアティヴを発揮することはできなかった。「想定外」の事態を想定するのは無理としても緊急事態に備えるシステムとルールを再検討する必要があるのではないだろうか。

Covid Measures and National Character

Japanese consensus tends to be based on precedent. When in doubt, look for a precedent and simply follow the previous methodology. However, if a major problem occurs and there is no precedent, then organizations seem unable to react quickly to solve the problem. When it becomes apparent that there is no contingency plan for solving a problem, they fall back on the notion of *soteigai*: "it was beyond all 5 expectations." In other words, they simply didn't imagine that such a thing could happen, so they had no emergency methods prepared ahead of time.

When the Covid epidemic first began, the air-tight "silos"—sectional divisions—of Japanese government ministries appeared incapable. They did not have precedent to fall back on and they did not seem capable of sharing information and working 10 across bureaucracies to reach an effective response.

For weeks, anxious Japanese struggled to obtain even a single protective mask, when it was clear that everyone needed them. So how could Japan, which was once admired for its just-in-time production methods, efficient delivery system, and high standard of living, not be able to immediately deliver large supplies of simple masks 15 to its citizens? Total quality control (TQC) seemed to belong to history.

● NOTES ●

1 **consensus**「コンセンサス、合意」／1 **precedent**「先例」／1 **in doubt**「疑わしい」／2 **methodology**「方法論」／4 **it becomes apparent that …** 文頭の it は仮主語で that 以下を指す。／4 **contingency**「不測の事態」／5 **fall back on**「を拠りどころにする」／7 **ahead of time**「あらかじめ、前もって」／8 **Covid** = Covid-19 ／8 **epidemic**「(感染症の) 流行」／8 **air-tight**「隙のない」／8 **silo**「サイロ」。飼料を貯蓄する円筒形の塔 ⇒「縦割り構造」／8 **sectional**「部門ごとの」／9 **incapable**「無能な」／11 **bureaucracy**「官僚制度、官僚機構」／12 **struggle to …**「…しようと努力する」／13 **how could Japan, …, not be able to** Japan の後から not の前までカンマで区切られた箇所は挿入句。／14 **just-in-time production method**「ジャスト・イン・タイム生産システム」。余剰を最低限まで減らして効率化された生産方式。トヨタの導入した方法として有名。／16 **total quality control**「統合的品質管理」。製品の品質を企画段階から部門横断的に管理するための方法。

✱ *Comprehension Check* ✱

1. Decision-making in Japan is dependent on . . .
   a. contingency planning.
   b. following precedents.
   c. preparing emergency methods.

38

The spread of the highly contagious virus showed another serious problem. Japan does not have a system for dealing with such extreme emergencies. Everything seems makeshift. The national government, under the Prime Minister exhibited little initiative in trying to clarify what was happening and establish effective policies for dealing with the constantly changing situation.   5

It quickly became clear that calling for "voluntary self-restraint," *jishuku*, was far from adequate. Political figures began calling for a change in the Constitution to allow for the declaration of a state of emergency. But there was resistance to that, and anyway, reaching a consensus on such a critical change in the basic law of the country would take a very long time. But why would the government not pass an emergency 10 measure, with a time limit, that would allow it to declare a state of emergency with specific levels of prohibited activities? Rather than looking around for someone to make a first move, someone in the government should have taken initiative. But no one seemed to have enough imagination to do that.

Instead, the Prime Minister's Cabinet and the country's prefectural governors 15 went back and forth regarding who should do what. No one seemed ready to declare a complete lockdown—with penalties for infringement—in order to gain some control over the worsening crisis. Instead, short-term restrictions were put into place, setting time limits and capacity limits for businesses, schools, and private gatherings. It was okay to drink alcohol in a restaurant until 7:00 p.m. but not after that. This made no 20 sense at all.

● NOTES ●

1 **contagious**「感染性の」／1 **virus**「ウィルス」／3 **makeshift**「その場しのぎ、間に合わせ」／3 **Prime Minister**「総理大臣、首相」／3 **little**「ほとんどない」／4 **initiative**「イニシアチブ、実行力」／4 **in trying to clarify … and establish …** clarify と establish が to 不定詞として並列されている。／4 **clarify**「を明らかにする」／6 **self-restraint**「自制」／7 **adequate**「充分である」／7 **political figure**「政治家」。cf. figure「人物」／7 **the Constitution**「憲法」／8 **declaration of a state of emergency**「緊急事態宣言」。cf. declaration「宣言、布告」／10 **take time**「時間がかかる」／10 **pass**「（法案を）可決する」／10 **emergency measure**「緊急措置」／11 **that** 直前の with a time limit は挿入句で、この that 以下の節は measure を後置修飾している。／12 **specific**「具体的な」／12 **prohibit**「を禁止する」／15 **the Cabinet**「内閣」。cf. cabinet「箪笥」／16 **go back and forth**「行ったり来たりする」／17 **lockdown**「封鎖」／17 **penalty**「罰則」／17 **infringement**「違反行為」／18 **worsen**「悪化する」／18 **be put into place**「が設置される」

✳ *Comprehension Check* ✳

2. Without systematic planning for emergencies, reactions may be . . .
   a. effective.
   b. clarified.
   c. makeshift.

3. Voluntary self-restraint proved to be . . .

    a. insufficient.

    b. prohibited.

    c. infringements.

The restaurant and *izakaya* trade suffered enormously. If there had been a sustained, complete shutdown until large portions of the population were vaccinated, then there could have been a gradual, continuous reopening of these businesses with safety for everyone. Instead, there were short-term, time-limited periods leading to lower figures of infections. Then as things reopened, the infection rates rose again. 5 This start-stop-start cycle repeated itself to the dismay of the public. Delays in vaccine distribution and in publicizing the times and places where vaccination was available left the public even more disgruntled.

It would be unfortunate if the various levels of government and the people themselves fail to learn from these experiences. There needs to be a deep discussion 10 and a rapid decision regarding the declaring of a state of emergency. Who can do it? How should it be enforced? What do you do with people who break restrictions? Japanese may be good at "voluntary self-restraint," but that is insufficient in events like the pandemic. Instead of worrying about the next election, politicians of all parties ought to collaborate in getting new expert information and laying down rules 15 so that there is no repeat of this incompetence in dealing with extreme conditions.

●NOTES●

1 **enormously**「非常に」／2 **sustained**「持続した」／2 **shutdown**「操業停止」／2 **vaccinate**「ワクチン接種をする」。cf. vaccine「ワクチン」／4 **lead to**「に至る」／5 **infection**「感染」／6 **dismay**「狼狽」／7 **distribution**「流通」／7 **publicize**「を広告する」／7 **where** 関係副詞。／8 **leave ~ ...**「~を…の状態に置いてゆく」この文の動詞は leave。／8 **disgruntled**「不満な」／12 **enforce**「施行する」／13 **insufficient**「不充分である」in- 否定の意、sufficient「充分である」／15 **party**「政党」／15 **collaborate**「協力する」／15 **lay down**「を制定する」／16 **incompetence**「無能力」in- 否定の意、competence「能力、適性」

✸Comprehension Check✸

4. According to the passage, people did not feel . . .

    a. delayed.

    b. dismayed.

    c. disgruntled.

5. To avoid a repeat of these experiences, the government ought to . . .

    a. declare a state of emergency.

    b. depend on self-restraint by the public.

    c. work to get expert opinions and set new rules.

❊ Structure Practice ❊

A. Choose the one underlined word or phrase that should be corrected or rewritten. Then change it so that the sentence is correct.

1. A responsible organization ₁should have contingency plans that can be ₂put to use ₃whenever an emergency ₄occur.   [   ]

2. Effective government ₁rely on dependable people in top positions, a willingness to ₂shift methods if necessary, and ₃a grasp of all the elements that ₄must be considered.   [   ]

B. Choose the word or phrase that best completes the sentence.

3. In the face of a medical emergency, government ministries ought to have experts with broad experience and dependable insight that they can . . . .
   a. deliver on   b. fall on   c. rely on   d. try on

4. In a rapidly changing situation it is understandably difficult to . . . measures that are both easy for the public to understand and easy to implement in various environments, such as congested cities and scattered farming areas.
   a. come up with   b. coping with   c. deal with   d. put up with

5. In order to effectively reduce the spread of Covid infections, both the government and the public strongly needs . . . updated information in order to make the correct decision about what to do.
   a. insufficient   b. sufficient   c. sustained   d. unsustainable

❊ Listening Challenge ❊

Listen and fill in the missing words.

1. It is ¹[   ] the national and prefectural governments were
   ²[   ] declare a complete lockdown because that ³[   ]
   every kind of business and people of all ages.

2. Despite ¹[   ] true experts in the field of medicine to tell the public
   what is happening ²[   ], some people turn to social media and
   listen instead to people ³[   ] to explain and recommend.

3. In order ¹[   ] emergencies, whether it be a pandemic or extreme
   weather conditions, it is our responsibility ²[   ] to
   protect ourselves as well as protect ³[   ].

4. If there is a kind of ¹[   ] about a topic, there is danger
   that people will ²[   ] pay attention to the important details but
   ³[   ].

5. It is ¹[   ] the successes and failures ²[   ]
   Covid will serve as precedents to remember ³[
               ] for future emergencies.

Going Further (for discussion or research)

1. In some countries, a "state of emergency" can be used to suppress public opinion
   and punish opponents of the government. Would having such a law in Japan have
   potential dangers?

2. How do you view the national and the Tokyo Metro governments' responses to the
   pandemic?

Foreign Technical Intern Trainees

外国人技能実習制度は1993年に創設され、本来は「国際協力・貢献」のための制度で、主に開発途上国の労働者を一定期間日本で受け入れ、技術や知識を学んでもらい、本国の発展に生かしてもらうことを目的としている。技能実習法には、基本理念として「技能実習は、労働力の需給の調整の手段として行われてはならない」と記されているが、実際には、日本の労働者不足を補うための制度という側面が強い。「国際貢献」を名目としながら、実態は、外国人を低賃金・単純労働力として受け入れるという構造的矛盾を抱えた制度を本格的に見直すのは、国際的な信用力を高めるためにも必須な課題ではないだろうか。

Foreign Technical Intern Trainees

🎧 41

In the past, Japan has kept its gates open to tourists who spend money and support the economy. But the country has kept its gates rather closed when it comes to immigrants who might take up residence permanently. While the average percentage of foreigners in the OECD nations is 12%, foreigners make up only 2% of the population in Japan.

But Japan is going to need workers from somewhere, very soon. Given the lack ⁵ of employees in elderly care facilities and childcare nurseries, the government should be more open to accepting mass immigration to counter the shrinking working-age population. The population of the country is dropping and it is anticipated that the working-age population (ages 15-65) will drop continually for the next decades. The Japanese government would be happy to increase the proportion of Japanese ¹⁰ women who work—at least in the lower-level, part-time or contract jobs—and keep all Japanese working later in life rather than expanding immigration. But that is not likely to solve the problem.

The government has made it easier for "trainees," or *kenshusei*, to come to Japan supposedly to gain skills to take back to their home countries after a period of three ¹⁵ or more years. This system suits the government because the incoming foreigners will not become permanent residents. They will come to Japan for a short time, provide labor, and return to their home countries. In return, the government claims, they will take home the skills they have gained in Japan.

●NOTES●

3 **take up**「取得する」／ 3 **residence**「居住権」／ 3 **permanently**「永遠の」permanent residence で「永住権」を表す。／ 4 **the OECD** = the Organisation for Economic Co-operation and Development「経済協力開発機構」／ 5 **Given**「を考慮すれば」／ 7 **mass immigration**「大量の移民」／ 8 **be anticipated**「予想される」cf. be expected ／ 11 **contract jobs**「契約社員」／ 12 **Japanese** = Japanese people ／ 14 **The government has made it easier … to Japan** 使役構文であり、for の目的語が to 以下の意味上の主語となる。it は to come 以下を表す。／ 15 **supposedly**「おそらく」／ 16 **suit**「にとって好都合である」

✳ *Comprehension Check* ✳

1. According to the passage, compared with other OECD nations, Japan . . .
   a. has a higher percentage of tourists.
   b. has six times more tourists than immigrants.
   c. economically benefits from foreign tourists.

2. The Japanese government seems to be . . .

   a. uninterested in putting Japanese women in the workplace.

   b. willing to have foreign workers for short periods of time.

   c. looking forward to a reduction of the country's population.

42

   In order to get to Japan, many trainees borrow money to pay commissions and deposits to related institutions in their home countries. In a survey in 2022, over 50% of responding interns said they had incurred debt in order to come to Japan. The average debt before departure to Japan was ¥547,799. Starting off in the red, they find it very hard to pay off the debt, much less save money from working in Japan.   5

   But the government quickly turns a blind eye to companies that exploit these visa bearers. Many trainees end up at jobs that offer little or no training and are little more than hard labor in forestry, farming, fishing, or food-processing jobs. The so-called trainees are forced to work long hours, are given little time off, and are punished if they become ill and cannot work. They have little or no contact with Japanese 10 people outside their workplaces and gain very little knowledge of Japanese language or Japan as a country. In effect, they are simply cheap labor and gain few skills to take home.

   They have little protection from abusive labor practices. The Japanese government, however, fails to check on the trainees or hold recruiting brokers or companies 15 accountable. The workers have no one to turn to for protection, even under normal conditions. Some employers do not even pay the minimum wage, and no one stops them from doing this.

●NOTES●

1 **commissions and deposits**「手数料や保証金」／3 **incur debt**「借金をする」／4 **in the red**「赤字で」／6 **turn a blind eye to**「に対して目をつむる」何かを無視するという意味になる。／6 **exploit**「搾取する」／6 **these visa bearers** = the trainees「これらのビザ取得者」／7 **end up** ~「結局~で終わる」／12 **in effect**「実質的に」／12 **cheap labor**「安価な労働力」／13 **abusive labor practices**「虐待的な労働の慣行」／14 **hold ~ accountable**「~に責任を持たせる」／14 **broker**「仲買人、ブローカー」／16 **the minimum wage**「最低賃金」cf. average, maximum.

✸ *Comprehension Check* ✸

3. In order to reach Japan some "trainees . . .

   a. have to borrow money.

   b. save money before leaving their home country.

   c. gain high-level Japanese language skills.

4. Some jobs which "trainees" do . . .

    a. are well-paid compared with jobs in their home countries.

    b. offer little training or no training at all.

    c. give them skills to take back to their own countries.

43

    Foreign workers depend more heavily on their employer than in other countries. Without help, they cannot get a mobile phone or open a bank account. In many cases, they need help getting housing. Many landlords refuse to rent housing to foreigners. The ones who are willing to rent to foreigners require a guarantor. All of this gives control to the employer.   5

    What's worse is that with the pandemic, many of these workers have lost their jobs. In some reported cases, they were not given wages that were due to be paid, were told to leave company dormitories, and received no assistance at all from the government. With no job, no place to live, and no money to pay for a plane ticket to their home country, they were stuck. Without assistance from charities, some ended 10 up in illegal businesses.

    While some migrant workers may come to Japan with naïve ideas about earning a lot to send home to their families, the Japanese government has a duty to ensure that the technical intern system is not abused. The government cannot simply continue to offer platitudes about "making concerted efforts to stamp out forced labor." It 15 must actually hold recruiters and employers accountable, and carefully monitor how migrant workers are treated.

●NOTES●

2 **Without help** = If there were no help; If it were not for help「補助なしでは」／3 **landlord**「大家さん」／4 **a guarantor**「保証人」／6 **the pandemic** ここでは 2020 年から続く、Covid-19 の世界的蔓延のことを指す。／8 **dormitory**「寮」／10 **be stuck**「身動きが取れない」／12 **naïve**「（考えなどが）甘い」日本語の「ナイーブ」とは意味が異なるため注意が必要。／15 **platitude**「決まり文句（中身の無い言葉）」／15 **concerted efforts**「協調努力」／15 **stamp out forced labor**「強制労働を根絶する」

✳Comprehension Check✳

5. These foreign workers . . .

    a. receive protection from the government while they are in Japan.

    b. often find the system of technical interns to be like forced labor.

    c. have no difficulty in finding housing and being paid regularly.

❊ Structure Practice ❊

A. Choose the one underlined word or phrase that should be corrected or rewritten. Then change it so that the sentence is correct.

1. While the government seems ₁aware that the country needs to ₂expand its work force, it remains ₃hesitant to allow more foreigners to come to Japan and ₄take in essential occupations.   [   ]

2. People who work ₁outside their own countries often need assistance with everyday ₂procedures they are ₃not used to and doing things in a foreign language is ₄challenge to say the least.   [   ]

B. Choose the word or phrase that best completes the sentence.

3. As children we . . . on our parents for our daily needs and other forms of support.
   a. check   b. depend   c. drop   d. gain

4. Because it was a holiday, everyone was traveling and we were . . . in traffic moving slower than someone on foot.
   a. blocked   b. incurred   c. shut   d. stuck

5. If it . . . your convenience, we could have lunch together on Friday.
   a. cares   b. keeps   c. seems   d. suits

❋ Listening Challenge ❋

🎧 **Listen and fill in the missing words.**

1. I felt ¹[   ] dropping rather quickly, ²[   ] was turning darker, and before long there was lightning and thunder; then ³[   ] like cats and dogs.

2. Our efforts ¹[   ] misinformation on social networks will only be successful ²[   ] realize who the real experts are and which people are ³[   ] attract attention.

3. Sarah was so picky about ¹[   ] she would eat, she ²[   ] the same restaurant ³[   ], because she liked their menu.

4. We discovered ¹[   ] of African art that people in their twenties ²[   ] of the visitors.

5. The next time I can ¹[   ], I would really ²[   ] a few days improving my gardening skills and ³[   ] to enjoy later.

Going Further (for discussion or research)

1. Should the government be responsible for protecting the rights of foreign workers with proper visas?

2. How long should foreign workers be allowed to work in Japan?

Financial Literacy

　日本には、お金に関してあまり細かい人間や、お金儲けのことばかり考えている人間を厭う文化が根強くある。しかし、現代は「武士は喰わねど高楊枝」的なやせ我慢が通用する時代ではとてもない。いまや労働者の所得水準は先進国の平均値より低くなってしまった。超低金利の時代は長く続き、預金金利は雀の涙にもならない、そんな中で数年前に政府は長寿時代の老後には2000万円の資産が必要と言った。高等学校の家庭課で「金融リテラシー」を扱うようになったが、「備えあれば憂いなし」の時代を生きるためには、家庭でも学校でもそれぞれの年齢でお金の感覚と知識を身につけさせる必要があるのだろうか。

Financial Literacy

45

Whether one calls it "financial literacy" or "personal finance," most Japanese would seem to need more of it. Perhaps there was little need for it in the past, but nowadays it is clear that everyone—at every stage of life—needs to know the basics.

As the current older generation of Japanese grew up, they could be fairly confident that if they worked hard, put money in postal savings or bank accounts, and paid into 5
the public pension system, they could rest easy. In the long run, they would have enough money to retire comfortably at 65 and not have to work again.

Several events have overturned that confidence. One is the economic downturn that resulted from the burst of the economic bubble. Some hard workers lost their full-time jobs and ended up as contract workers at lower pay. They were willing to work 10
hard, but there were few well-paying jobs on offer. Even if one already had a regular job, there was virtually no increase in monthly pay, once inflation had been taken into consideration.

Another event is the decrease in interest rates on savings accounts. In the 1980s, time deposits were paying as much as 8% interest, but interest rates eventually began 15
to slide downward. Now they are less than 0.1%. For those who were used to just "putting extra money in the bank"—or in a hiding place at home—that money didn't increase. Afraid to invest money in stocks or bonds, they just assumed that they would have "enough" to add to pension payments. Their parents had done that, so things would work out. 20

●NOTES●

1 **financial literacy**「金融に関する知識、金融リテラシー」／2 **need more of it** it = "financial literacy" or "personal finance" が、より必要であるという意味。目的語 it の直前に of が必要である点に注意。／5 **postal savings**「郵便貯金（複数形）」／6 **the public pension system**「公的年金制度」／8 **a downturn**「不況」／9 **the burst of the economic bubble**「バブル崩壊」。ここでは日本における 1991 年のバブル崩壊を指す。／10 **contract worker**「契約社員」／14 **interest rate**「金利」／15 **time deposit**「定期預金、積立貯金」／18 **stocks or bonds**「株（通例複数形）もしくは債券」／20 **work out**「うまくいく、なんとかなる」

✳ *Comprehension Check* ✳

1. According to the passage, education in financial literacy . . .

   a. seems necessary for all age groups today.

   b. can be limited to schools.

   c. would be most helpful to those who are retiring.

2. One economic event that has not occurred is . . .

    a. jobs that pay well have increased.

    b. interest rates at banks have decreased.

    c. homes have become easier to buy.

46   A third event was the report issued by the Financial Services Agency in 2019, which was a wake-up call for many older citizens. Japanese were living longer, and if a couple lived to the age of 95, they would need at least ¥20 million in assets. Relying solely on public pension benefits would definitely not cover the cost of living post-retirement. After watching their own parents retire at 65, they were faced with 5 working much longer—not for luxuries but just for basic living expenses.

    A large percentage of people in their 20s to 50s are now wishing they had developed financial literacy earlier in life. At present, some 54% of total household financial assets is concentrated in cash, or basic savings accounts. Only 16% is in bonds, stocks, and mutual funds. The mind-set that investments are risky and that 10 cash is the safest strategy has proven hard to change. Furthermore, until now in Japan it has seemed like a taboo to talk about money in school and even at home.

    In other countries, however, schools are taking several initiatives. The Australian government has introduced a strategy to promote financial education in both lower grades and high school education. England's national curriculum includes budgeting, 15 risk management, and financial services and products.

●NOTES●

1 **the Financial Services Agency**「金融庁」／2 **a wake-up call**「警鐘」モーニングコールの意味もある。／ 2 **Japanese** = Japanese people ／3 **asset**「資産」／6 **luxuries**「贅沢（品）」単数形は luxury で「贅沢品」 や「贅沢（不可算用法）」などの意味がある。／10 **mutual fund**「投資信託」／10 **mind-set**「考え方、物の 見方、マインドセット」／12 **a taboo**「禁忌、タブー」／13 **initiative**「主導権、イニシアチブ」／15 **budgeting, risk management, and financial services and products**「予算の編成、リスクの管理、金融サービスや金融 商品」

✳Comprehension Check✳

3. Public pension benefits . . .

    a. were at one time considered sufficient for post-retirement needs.

    b. should be replaced by purchasing bonds and stocks.

    c. are reduced as people grow older.

4. It seems that to most Japanese . . .

    a. discussing retirement ages is considered taboo.

    b. basic savings accounts are the most common way to save for retirement.

    c. investments are the safest strategy for saving money.

47

    Home economics teachers in senior high schools in Japan are now dealing with financial literacy in the curriculum. The aim is not to tell students that saving is a bad choice. The aim is to teach them how to handle unexpected financial shocks and to think about various options, so they can make the decisions for themselves. Some home economics teachers are worried that they don't have enough expertise 5 to properly teach students. In addition, classroom time is already jam-packed with material to cover. This is where a "special subject teacher," perhaps one with experience in finance, could be of great assistance.

    Both families and schools need to promote "money sense" at each age level. At the very least, learning about the cost of living, balancing a budget, keeping track of 10 interest on savings, and understanding the risks of credit cards should be something young people should learn early on.

    When one has enough money to pay the bills for one month, it is tempting to overlook what might happen in the long run. But when something unexpected comes along—like a pandemic—it shows how important it is to plan ahead, for next year, 15 and for the rest of your life.

●NOTES●

1 **Home economics**「家庭科」／3 **unexpected financial shock**「予期せぬ経済的な打撃」cf. expect「予期する」／5 **expertise**「専門知識」／6 **jam-packed**「すし詰めの」／7 **special subject teacher**「特別教科担当教員」／9 **money sense**「お金に関する感覚」／14 **in the long run**「長い目で見ると」／15 **a pandemic**「感染症などの大流行」

✳ *Comprehension Check* ✳

5. In senior high schools in Japan, teaching financial literacy is . . .

    a. easy for home economics teachers to teach.

    b. going to be taught by special subject teachers.

    c. a means of helping students make their own decisions.

❊ Structure Practice ❊

A. Choose the one underlined word or phrase that should be corrected or rewritten. Then change it so that the sentence is correct.

1. ₁<u>Upon hearing</u> the ₂<u>loud crash</u> of a traffic accident, I ₃<u>jumped to</u> my feet, ₄<u>overturned</u> my chair.   [   ]

2. Our goal in ₁<u>set up</u> a tutoring program for ₂<u>less-fortunate</u> students is ₃<u>to help them with</u> their studies ₄<u>prior to</u> entrance examinations.   [   ]

B. Choose the word or phrase that best completes the sentence.

3. There's no guarantee that my application to study abroad will be accepted, but for the time being, I'm just hoping that things will . . . out so I can continue my studies.
   a. clear   b. help   c. rest   d. work

4. My family's estimates of how much our living costs are per month have . . . to be pretty accurate.
   a. proof   b. prove   c. proven   d. proving

5. One fundamental routine in personal finances is to . . . the balance in your bank account and your credit card statements.
   a. invest in   b. keep track of   c. take risks with   d. wake up to

❊ Listening Challenge ❊

Listen and fill in the missing words.

48

1. Discussing ¹[   ] family budgets is ²[   ] children learn how to handle expenses ³[   ] and become independent.

2. ¹[   ], it was considered a rule of thumb that ²[

       ] what one did not have, but credit cards ³[   ] to

   "buy now and pay later."

3. High school teachers ¹[   ] having to teach a

   complicated subject which they are ²[   ], so having someone

   with financial experience come in ³[   ] helpful.

4. The ¹[   ] interest rates is of particular ²[

          ] who is planning to buy a condominium, because the fixed rate of a

   30-year loan ³[   ] his or her lifestyle for three full

   decades.

5. Ultimately, ¹[   ] individual how much risk the person is willing

   to take ²[   ] investments in bonds and stocks, but having basic

   understanding of such assets ³[   ] such decisions.

Going Further (for discussion or research)

1. A few people think that cryptocurrencies, for example Bitcoin, are good investments.
   What do you think about these financial instruments?

2. Do you believe that one day in the future cash will disappear and we will all use
   digital money? Why or why not?

CHAPTER *13* 地方移住

Heading to the Country

地方に移住してスローライフを楽しむ人びとはコロナ感染が流行する前からいた。しかし、以前は退職後の田舎暮らしを楽しむという人たちが一般的であった。コロナ禍によるリモートワークが契機になったこともあるのだろうが、今、積極的に地方への移住を実行したり模索したりしている人びとがいる。受け入れる側も寂れていく地域社会の活性化のために、新しい住民に期待するところは大きく、定住化のためのさまざまな方策を講じている。こうした動きは人口の都市集中を減らすことに貢献するのだろうか。

Heading to the Country

49
Over several decades, a consistent demographic trend has been for Japanese young people to leave the countryside and head for the cities. Farming has not been an attractive occupation and the jobs and bright lights of the city have had considerable appeal. Net emigration from the countryside to Tokyo, Osaka, and other urban centers has risen consistently. As the populations of metropolitan areas have climbed, those 5 of rural communities have declined, and the average age of people remaining in the countryside has risen.

But a recent phenomenon suggests that times may have changed. Even before the Covid pandemic and the increase in remote work options, some city-dwellers have headed in the reverse direction. 10

In earlier times, it was usually retired people who left crowded urban areas to enjoy a slower pace in the country. Some returned to their childhood home. Others began by buying a weekend and vacation home. After they tested the waters of the slow life, they decided to give up their city residence and move to the countryside to live fulltime. 15

●NOTES●
1 **demographic**「人口統計学的な」／4 **Net emigration**「純移動民」／5 **metropolitan areas**「大都市圏」／6 **rural communities**「地方（圏）」cf. urban areas／9 **city-dwellers**「都市生活者」／12 **Some** = Some people／13 **test the water(s) of**「の様子をみる」／15 **fulltime**「全時間」ここでは生活の拠点を本格的に田舎に移すことを意味する。

✽ *Comprehension Check* ✽

1. One phenomenon that has not occurred is . . .

   a. some retired people have moved into the countryside.

   b. rural populations have risen.

   c. emigration to major urban centers has continued to rise.

50
Now, however, there is another group of emigrants from the urban centers. This group is composed of younger singles, couples, and even families, without local connections. They begin by contacting the NGO Furusato Kaiki Shien Center, an organization which supports people who want to move to rural areas. Recently, towns in Kagawa, Yamanashi, Ehime, and Fukushima prefectures have worked with this 5

NGO to appeal to young people who are tired of city life. The organization advertises organizations in these prefectures that are eager and willing to accept new residents to revitalize their local communities.

Interest in rural areas has been boosted by young people re-evaluating their lives, looking for peace and quiet, a cheaper lifestyle, a better work-life balance, and perhaps participation in a local community. 10

Of course, some of these "migrants" bring their jobs with them. If there is dependable broadband internet service available, those who do most of their work online can avoid long daily commutes on crowded subways and trains and escape from cramped apartments. These online nomads can turn on their devices anywhere 15 and be ready to work. When needed, dependable home delivery services allow overnight deliveries of necessary equipment, supplies, and devices. These services also guarantee access to almost anything one could want from a company in a city. As long as they complete their daily quota, they are then free to go for walks in the countryside, fish in local streams, and buy local produce from their farming neighbors. 20

●NOTES●

3 **the NGO** = Non-governmental Organization「非政府組織」のこと。／6 **appeal to**「（心に）訴える、にアピールする」／8 **revitalize**「復興させる、活性化させる」／9 **boost**「増加させる」／13 **broadband**「広帯域通信の、ブロードバンドの」／15 **cramped**「手狭な」／15 **nomad**「ノマド」遊牧民を意味する nomad であるが、ここでは「特定の場所を持たずに仕事をする人々」を指す。／19 **quota**「割り当て、ノルマ」／20 **stream**「小川」

✳ *Comprehension Check* ✳

2. Furusato Kaiki Shien Center is an organization that . . .
   a. links young urbanites with people in rural areas.
   b. finds workers for farmers.
   c. provides jobs to young farming families.

3. Among the services young "migrants" to the countryside do not find essential is . . .
   a. stable internet connections.
   b. dependable delivery services.
   c. cramped living quarters.

Other migrants have completely broken from their former urban lives. They have left unsatisfying occupations and—often with the tutoring of local people who are willing to teach them—have actually taken up farming. They may start off with just enthusiasm and no know-how at all, but by showing a willingness to learn, their new neighbors may prove extremely kind in sharing what they have learned over a lifetime ⁵ of farming. The relationship has to be reciprocal, but if it is, the new connection is a win-win proposition.

Though probably fewer in number, still others move to the countryside to devote their energies to learning traditional crafts. There are skills in weaving, dyeing, pottery, lacquerware, and other handcrafts that are disappearing due to the out-migration of ¹⁰ young people. But with the proper show of respect, a desire to learn, and the promise of long-term dedication, a relative amateur can develop skills. The craftsman gains a successor, and the novice gains a new career.

This trend is encouraging to towns and villages that once seemed headed for extinction. The sparsely populated town of Shimanto, in the island of Shikoku, for ¹⁵ example, offers subsidies for housing and child care for the newly arrived. It seems that the new residents are undeterred by the lack of infrastructure in the countryside. Instead they are attracted by the helpfulness of the local people and the sense of belonging to a community.

● NOTES ●

1 **break from**「から脱却する」／2 **tutor**「教える」。名詞としては「家庭教師」などの意味もある。／4 **know-how**「ノウハウ」／6 **reciprocal**「相互的な」／7 **proposition**「命題」という意味もあるが、ここでは「提案、申し入れ」の意味が適切。／9 **crafts**「工芸」／9 **weaving, dyeing, pottery, lacquerware …**「織物、染物、陶芸、漆器」／10 **out-migration**「人口流出」／13 **the novice**「初心者」／16 **subsidies**「補助金」subsidy の複数形である。／17 **undeterred**「思い止まらされていない、引き止められていない」

✳ *Comprehension Check* ✳

4. Some young migrants from urban centers have . . .

    a. teaching in local schools.

    b. taken up farming occupations.

    c. taught local farmers better types of agriculture.

5. Learning traditional crafts from people in the countryside . . .

    a. helps older craftspeople develop someone to take over the craft.

    b. enables younger people to learn a craft to take back to the cities.

    c. can be done in exchange for child care for the new arrivals.

❀ Structure Practice ❀

A. Choose the one underlined word or phrase that should be corrected or rewritten. Then change it so that the sentence is correct.

1. While the children of some farmers have ₁turned their backs agriculture as an occupation that ₂carries risks of weather disasters and ₃financial burdens, some outsiders have chosen farming as a lifestyle for ₄completely different reasons.

    [   ]

2. Attaining skill in traditional crafts ₁is often said require ten years, so ₂it demands considerable determination and commitment to continue ₃learning the fundamentals and then the ₄fine points of a particular craft.   [   ]

B. Choose the word or phrase that best completes the sentence.

3. The slower pace of country life and the stronger sense of community in the countryside definitely . . . to people who are tired of the stressful life of the urban areas.

    a. appeals   b. encourages   c. matches   d. promises

4. There needs to be a . . . relation of trust, enthusiasm, and dedication to learning between a master craftsperson and a novice learner.

    a. access   b. necessary   c. reciprocal   d. subsidy

5. Starting a new life in a new country didn't . . . many Japanese soccer players from moving to Germany, England, and Italy to play for new teams.

    a. deter   b. force   c. make   d. guarantee

✳ Listening Challenge ✳

 Listen and fill in the missing words.

1. It is ¹[   ] workers who have grown tired of the daily
   commute to work ²[   ] and worked beyond regular office
   hours ³[   ] an alternative way to earn a living.

2. With ¹[   ], the necessary devices, and a ²[
                    ], nomad workers are no longer tied to a city office, and ³[
                    ] as a workplace.

3. More than one NGO ¹[   ] assistance to would-be
   "migrants" who ²[   ] a cheaper lifestyle and a slower
   pace but also an opportunity to become part of a community ³[
             ] in urban areas.

4. Among the great appeals of ¹[   ] are the traditional
   crafts of the so-called Mingei Movement ²[   ] including
   Yanagi Soetsu, who found beauty ³[   ] that are made
   by hand by unknown craftspeople.

5. Midway through the game, our team ¹[   ] another loss, but
   we scored one goal, then another, and ²[   ] our energy came back
   and ³[   ] and win the game 5 to 4.

Going Further (for discussion or research)

1. In your own view, what are the appeals of urban life and country life?

2. Is there any kind of traditional Japanese craft that you might be interested in
   learning?

Does Dedication Require Overtime?

少子化が進むにあたって今後ますます深刻になる労働力不足を背景に、政府が音頭を取って、時間外労働の上限は月 45 時間かつ年 360 時間が原則、有給休暇の義務化、パートタイム労働者の待遇改善などを盛り込んだ「働き方改革関連法案」が 2019 年の 4 月から施行された。しかし、労働現場の現実は理想とはほど遠く、「過労死」のニュースは後を絶たない。少ない労働人口で高い生産性をキープするという理想を現実のものとするには、雇用する側とされる側の両者が納得できる改革への道のりは遠いのだろうか。

Does Dedication Require Overtime?

🎧
53

Japan brought about its postwar economic boom through a tough bargain. Companies agreed to look after their employees for life in exchange for a willingness to dedicate their entire careers to the company. For the companies, it was risky to keep everyone on the payrolls, even during a business downturn, but it was basically successful as a strategy. For the employees, however, it involved a series of sacrifices. 5 Sacrifice home life for late hours at the office, working overtime. Sacrifice relations with spouse and children, by being transferred to another city, while the other members of the family stayed in the original home. Work hard now for a guaranteed future in the company.

Until now the emphasis in such enterprises has been on "harmony" and 10 "cooperation" in the workplace. Employees have hesitated to leave the office before their bosses, and even before their peers. Leaving first, they think, would be rude, inconsiderate, or disloyal. But hours in the office—or calling on clients—were not always examples of efficiency. If everyone was efficient—like the Danes and the Swedes—everyone should have been able to go home by 6:00, to have dinner with 15 their families.

So it has been somewhat surprising that the Japanese central government noticed that Kasumigaseki was becoming less attractive to university graduates looking for jobs. It seems that the appeal of a career civil servant position has worn off a bit. The immediate cause of this awakening was the fact that bureaucrats are sensitive 20 to numbers, especially budget funding. When increases in overtime pay went up, the government needed to know why.

●NOTES●
1 **bring about**「をもたらす」brought about はその過去形。／1 **a tough bargain**「難しい交渉」／4 **payroll**「給与台帳、従業員名簿」ここでは、on the payrolls で「雇用されている」という意味になる。／4 **a downturn**「不況」／7 **spouse**「配偶者」／10 **enterprise**「企業」他に「企て」という意味もある。／12 **a peer**「仲間、同僚」／13 **disloyal**「不誠実な」／14 **the Danes and the Swedes**「デンマーク人とスウェーデン人」／19 **wear off**「徐々に消える、薄れていく」／20 **this awakening**「(直前の文の内容を指して) この気付き」／20 **a bureaucrat**「官僚、役人」

✻Comprehension Check✻

1. The postwar economic boom in Japan . . .
   a. required workers to take lots of risks.
   b. depended on companies giving lifetime employment.
   c. had nothing to do with guarantees for futures in the companies.

80   Chapter 14

2. Long hours in the office . . .

   a. were supposed to show loyalty to the company.

   b. were examples of efficient working habits.

   c. have encouraged university graduates to work in the central government.

54

    The government, like private companies, has seemed unmoved by calls for reform and reduction of overtime work. To the contrary, until recently, they have their employees do "service" overtime—*sabisu zangyo*—which is actually "overtime without pay." But the fact that an increasing number of civil servants quit their jobs and fewer people apply for jobs is a signal that something isn't working right. Employees 5 may have done unpaid overtime to show loyalty, dedication, and determination in the past, but as the unpaid load has increased, the appeal of having such a position has been tarnished.

    In contrast to this is the issue of whether these "hard workers" are actually accomplishing much. If they increased their productivity and efficiency, some claim, 10 there would be no reason to stay beyond the regular working hours. By eliminating unnecessary paperwork and digitalizing many procedures, there would be less need for employees to stay late to deal with documents and communications.

●NOTES●

1 **a call for**「（を求める）要請」ここでは、calls for reform and reduction of overtime work で「時間外労働の削減や改革を求める声」という意味になる。／6 **loyalty, dedication, and determination**「忠誠心、献身、決意」／8 **tarnished**　ここでは「損なわれた」という意味で、他に「色褪せた」などの意味もある。／12 **digitalize**「デジタル化する」

✳ *Comprehension Check* ✳

3. Increased efficiency could contribute to . . .

   a. fewer civil servants.

   b. less unpaid overtime work.

   c. reduced paperwork.

Paying workers for performance rather than seniority would be a start in solving this problem. Why pay an inefficient employee who works from 8:30 into the evening the same as a highly efficient employee who works from 8:30 to 5:30 and goes home on time? Is the judgment on efficiency left up to a manager who is not keeping track of the productivity of his subordinates but only checking how many hours they are in the office?

Another fundamental question that governments and companies never seem to address is why is overtime necessary. Instead of causing their employees to develop unhealthy routines, why don't employers hire more employees and let everyone go home before 6:00?

The Diet has passed a law that limits overtime to a maximum of 100 hours per month. But think about it this way: 100 hours is roughly two 50-hour workweeks. That means squeezing six weeks of work into a four-week month. It may be reasonable to ask employees to work a few hours extra during one week on occasion, but not 25 extra hours a week on a regular basis.

All the while, companies have refused to hire additional full-time employees. Instead, they have used a system that allows contracted employees, who they can hire with no promise of a later promotion to full-time status. These workers do the job of regular employees, at usually less than half of the salary, and are released just prior to the date when they would have to be given full-time status under the law.

●NOTES●

1 **seniority**「年功序列」／4 **leave up to**「に任せる」／4 **keep track of**「を記録する、追跡する、把握する」／5 **a subordinate**「部下」／9 **unhealthy routines**「不健康な日常生活」ここでは習慣化する時間外労働のことを意味する。／11 **100 hours per month**「ひと月あたり100時間」perには「あたり」という意味がある。ひと月あたり100時間というのは、臨時的に労使が協定で結ぶことが出来る、時間外労働と休日労働を合計した時間の上限である。／13 **squeeze**「詰め込む」他には「絞る」などの意味もある。／17 **contracted employees**「契約社員」／19 **prior to**「に先立って、より前に」

✳ *Comprehension Check* ✳

4. Among the solutions to reducing overtime work is . . .
   a. increasing the number of full-time employees.
   b. more dependence on seniority.
   c. improving healthy routines.

5. According to the passage, requiring as many as 100 hours of overtime per month is . . .

    a. efficient.

    b. occasional.

    c. unreasonable.

❈ Structure Practice ❈

A. Choose the one underlined word or phrase that should be corrected or rewritten. Then change it so that the sentence is correct.

1. Given that the central government and major private corporations require ₁significantly overtime work, it ₂should come as no surprise that such positions are no longer as ₃attractive to university graduates as they ₄used to be.

    [   ]

2. One wonders ₁whether putting in long hours at the office is ₂equivalent to being productive and efficient, or whether overtime hours ₃indicates a lack of ₄such qualities.   [   ]

B. Choose the word or phrase that best completes the sentence.

3. Achieving one's career goal . . . a clear understanding of the skills that one needs to obtain and a realistic view of the likelihood of reaching that target.

    a. concerns   b. follows   c. requires   d. takes

4. Employers seem to take it for granted that workers are willing to work overtime without being paid for extra hours and to . . . overtime day after day, not just on occasion.

    a. prior to   b. put in   c. take in   d. work out

5. Our boss is quite sensitive to criticism so we are hesitant . . . mention any she makes or point out something she misunderstands.

    a. about   b. for   c. regarding   d. to

❋ Listening Challenge ❋

56 🎧 **Listen and fill in the missing words.**

1. While ¹[   ] my boss by getting my job done quickly, I
   ²[   ] that it only resulted in my ³[   ] extra
   work to do.

2. Repeated failures ¹[   ] for emergencies and ²[
             ] quickly will tarnish ³[   ].

3. You ¹[   ] the physical and ²[   ] employees
   would be ³[   ] of any large organization.

4. When an employee ¹[   ] that he or she is experiencing
   burnout and that there are ²[   ] elsewhere, it makes
   sense ³[   ] changing jobs.

5. The use of ¹[   ], who are paid ²[   ]
   workers, has ³[   ] Japanese businesses and
   government offices.

Going Further (for discussion or research)

1. Imagining that you and your spouse both work from 8:30 to 5:30. Would you
   be eager to have children, depend on child care *hoikusho*, and share household
   cleaning and cooking chores?

2. Is it acceptable to force employees to work overtime every day?

Refugee Status

日本の入管（出入国在留管理局）は審査が厳しいことで知られるが、収容されていた外国人が死亡した。「難民条約」の下で、難民の認定を受けた外国人は、原則として締約国の国民あるいは一般外国人と同じように待遇され、我が国においても日本国民と同じ待遇を受けることができる。ウクライナ難民に関しては政府は比較的寛容な政策を取っているが、日本で難民認定されることは極めて厳しい。日本の難民認定が少なすぎることについては、「審査をきちんとやった結果だ」という声もあるが、「助けを求めて逃れてきた難民が現実に助けられていないという」人道上の問題をどう考えれば良いのだろうか。

Refugee Status

57

It is estimated that some 82,000 foreigners are illegally overstaying in Japan. These foreigners may have entered Japan on a tourist visa or a working visa and have stayed beyond the time limit stated on that visa. In a sense, they simply "disappear" and law enforcement agencies do not know where they are. One assumes that they have found some kind of work to support themselves, but also suspects that some of 5 these overstayers are working at illegal jobs.

If the government is able to locate one of these people, it issues a deportation order. On an annual basis, some 10,000 foreigners return to their countries after receiving these orders, but another 3,000 remain in Japan.

A separate category of foreigners come to Japan because they fear for their lives 10 if they stay in their native country. They are afraid that they will be put in prison, tortured, or even executed due to their political activities or even lifestyle issues. Proving that they are endangered if they return, they apply for asylum as refugees. But the Japanese government does not grant asylum easily.

●NOTES●

1 **some** = about ／4 **law enforcement agency** 「法執行機関」広義における、保安官や警察のことを表す。／ 6 **these overstayers** は2行目の These foreigners を指す。「不法長期滞在者」／ 7 **issue** 「（命令を）出す」／ 7 **a deportation order** 「強制退去の命令」／ 11 **a native country** 「母国」／ 12 **execute** 「処刑する」／ 14 **grant** 「許可を与える」／ 14 **asylum** 「亡命」

✳Comprehension Check✳

1. Those who fear they will be punished if they return to their native countries are called . . .

    a. overstayers.

    b. refugees.

    c. asylums.

These self-declared "refugees" may make repeated applications for asylum, because that automatically allows them to stay while their applications are processed. The issue of asylum received serious attention in March 2021 with the death, while being detained by immigration authorities, of Wishima Rathnayake, from Sri Lanka. After her repeated requests for release for medical treatment at a hospital were denied by authorities, she died alone in her cell at the age of 33.

Application for asylum may seem like little more than a strategy for remaining in Japan. However, for a significant portion of these applicants, there is a real danger that if they were forced to return to their home countries, their lives would be endangered. The danger could be due to their religious beliefs, their political activities, or ethnic conflict. The danger is particularly acute when the home country is in turmoil. Refugees from certain countries in the Sahel in Africa and the Middle East are entirely justified in fearing for their lives if they return.

Among those who are currently seeking legal refuge in Japan are citizens of Myanmar who have come to Japan with legitimate visas as students and trainees. Due to the government takeover in their home country during their absence, some have participated in legal protests in Japan and their names and photos are in the public domain. They fear that they will be taken into custody if they return. As a result, they have no alternatives other than to apply for asylum or simply "disappear."

● NOTES ●

1 **self-declared**「自ら宣言した」／4 **detained**「拘留される」／4 **immigration authorities**「入国監査官」 cf. Immigration Bureau「入国管理局」、Immigration Services Agency「出入国在留管理庁」／6 **a cell**「独房」他には「細胞」などの意味もある。／10 **religious beliefs**「宗教上の信条」／11 **ethnic conflict**「民族的な対立」／11 **acute**「深刻な」／11 **in turmoil**「混乱の中にある」／15 **legitimate visas**「正規の査証 (ビザ)」／16 **the government takeover**「(クーデターなどによる) 政権の交代」／17 **in the public domain**「公知となっている」。ここでは「メディア等を通じて広く知られてしまっている」状態を表現している。／18 **taken into custody**「身柄を拘束される」

✽ Comprehension Check ✽

2. Those who apply for asylum . . .
   a. are only trying to remain in Japan.
   b. may be in danger if they return to their home countries.
   c. have no reason to avoid deportation.

3. Those who apply for legal refuge in Japan . . .

    a. may have come to Japan with a student visa.

    b. are all from Africa and the Middle East.

    c can make only one application.

      The United Nations High Commissioner for Refugees (UNHCR) has criticized
Japan for its actions toward such refugees. UN experts say Japan's current policies
and proposed revisions fail to meet international standards from the standpoint of
human rights.

      At present, Japan accepts only roughly 1% of the applications it receives. In 2020,   5
the government certified only 47 applications out of 3,936 that were submitted. By
international standards, this is outrageously low. A proposed law would make it even
harder for applicants to succeed. A foreigner who has applied for refugee status three
times and been denied that status could be deported. The person would be put on a
plane to return to their home country, with no regard to what might happen when they 10
arrive.

      On the positive side, Japan has agreed to take in refugees from Ukraine who have
relatives in Japan. This is certainly commendable, given the serious humanitarian
crisis in that country. However, how does one explain this special treatment to
foreigners who claim their lives would be endangered if they returned to their home 15
countries, countries other than Ukraine? Will people from other violent territories be
granted the same refugee status?

●NOTES●

1 **The United Nations High Commissioner for Refugees (UNHCR)**「国連難民高等弁務官事務所」／
3 **the standpoint of human rights**「人権の観点から」／6 **certify**「認定する」／7 **outrageously**「法外
に」outrageous には「凶暴な」や「途方も無い」など複数の意味があるため注意。／9 **deported**「強制送還
される」。cf. deportation ／10 **with no regard to**「を気にもせず、を顧慮せずに」= without regard to ／13
commendable「称賛に値する」／13 **the serious humanitarian crisis**「深刻な人道的危機」／16 **violent**
territories「戦域、紛争地域」／17 **grant**「与える」

� *Comprehension Check* ✹

4. The United Nations High Commissioner for Refugees claims . . .

    a. Japan's policies toward refugees are too loose.

    b. Japan's policies toward applicants is quite fair.

    c. Japan's policies do not match international standards.

5. Japan's policies toward Ukraine refugees with relatives in Japan . . .

   a. is admirable.

   b. represents its policies toward applicants from all countries.

   c. is only a short-term policy and will be changed later.

❊ Structure Practice ❊

A. Choose the one underlined word or phrase that should be corrected or rewritten. Then change it so that the sentence is correct.

1. If a foreigner wishes ₁to stay in Japan longer than the time limit ₂stated on a visa, the person is required to ₃apply for an extension of that visa ₄prior that date.

   [   ]

2. The government ₁appears to have rather vague standards for determining the ₂standards by which applicants for refugee status ₃has a real reason to fear for personal safety upon being ₄forced to return to their home country.

   [   ]

B. Choose the word or phrase that best completes the sentence.

3. His success as a Nordic skier is . . . the physical conditioning he maintains throughout the year.

   a. because of   b. due to   c. out of   d. regardless of

4. We began planning our trip six months ago, and we thought we had everything worked out, but we . . . notice that many of the places we intended to visit were closed on Mondays, so we didn't get to see everything we had planned to.

   a. hoped to   b. applied to   c. failed to   d. submitted to

5. The group has applied for permission to take photos in the museum, and if permission is . . . they will all bring their cameras.

   a. denied   b. endangered   c. enforced   d. granted

❊ Listening Challenge ❊

🎧 **Listen and fill in the missing words.**

1. The company ¹[   ] it will take 10 workdays ²[
   ] and another 3 workdays to run tests ³[   ] works
   properly.

2. After surgery, ¹[   ] in the hospital for further medical
   treatment, and once ²[   ], he will be released and
   ³[   ] his routine.

3. The public is frustrated by ¹[   ] certain kinds of medicines
   and insufficient and ²[   ] regarding the best way ³[
   ] the current situation.

4. For people in many countries ¹[   ] how one could be
   endangered if one's religious beliefs ²[   ] that of other
   people or if there is conflict ³[   ] origins.

5. If you ¹[   ] for the position by the end of this month,
   you will ²[   ] by the 10th of next month ³[   ].

Going Further (for discussion or research)

1. Why is Japan so reluctant to approve refugee status to foreigners?

2. What could be done to help refugees get started in making a new life in Japan?

Japan's Dilemmas and Solutions
15 Topics You Need to Consider
考えよう日本の論点15

編著者	James M. Vardaman
	鎌 田 明 子
	岡 田 大 樹
	小 林 亮 一 朗
発行者	山 口 隆 史

発 行 所　　　　株式会社 音羽書房鶴見書店

〒113-0033　東京都文京区本郷 3-26-13
TEL 03-3814-0491
FAX 03-3814-9250
URL: https://www.otowatsurumi.com
e-mail: info@otowatsurumi.com

2023 年 3 月 1 日　　初版発行
2023 年 4 月 10 日　　2 刷発行

組版・装幀　ほんのしろ
印刷・製本　（株）シナノ
■ 落丁・乱丁本はお取り替えいたします。

E-149